Entertaining an Artist

Vegan. Wheatfree. Handful!

Jacky Francis Walker

Written in this house... about events that happened in + around! Part of the house's history. Here's to its next incarnation. Enjoy being here

Jacky Francis Walker 2020

This entirely scurrilous, scandalous, fiction should never have found its way into print!

'An Artist'

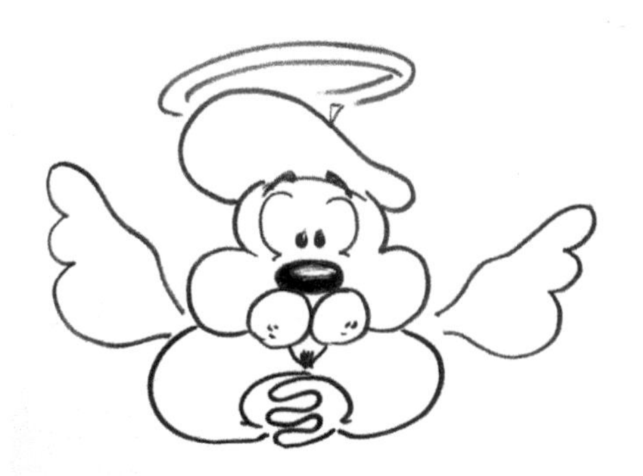

First published in Great Britain in 2018 by Bonobo TV
www.bonobo.tv

ISBN - 978-1-907729-26-3

Edited by Geoff Francis

Illustrated by Carolynn de Waal

Designed by Paul Windridge

Printed and bound in Great Britain by
Lightning Source (UK) Ltd, London

www.lightningsource.com

Entertaining an Artist

Vegan. Wheatfree. Handful!

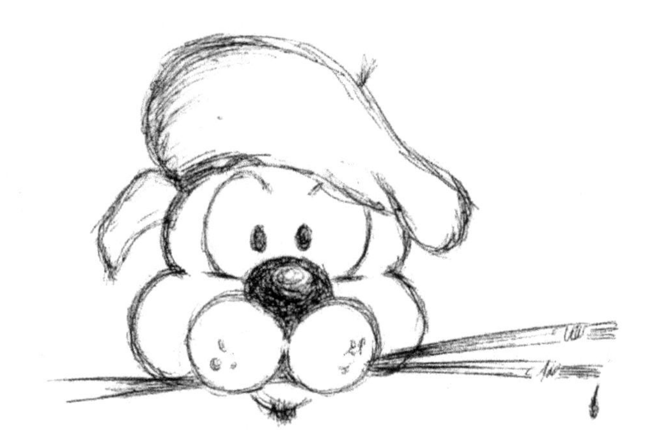

Entertaining an Artist

The Artist is busy eating... And I - again - cooked. Shopped. Cleared up.

But the notion has come for me to write a book.

Entertaining an Artist.

And through this story, you'll be able to see how it unfolds. And enjoy the food journey too. It just happens to be vegan food, wheat free too. But the most important thing is that food should be good enough for anyone to enjoy, no matter what their tastes or persuasions.

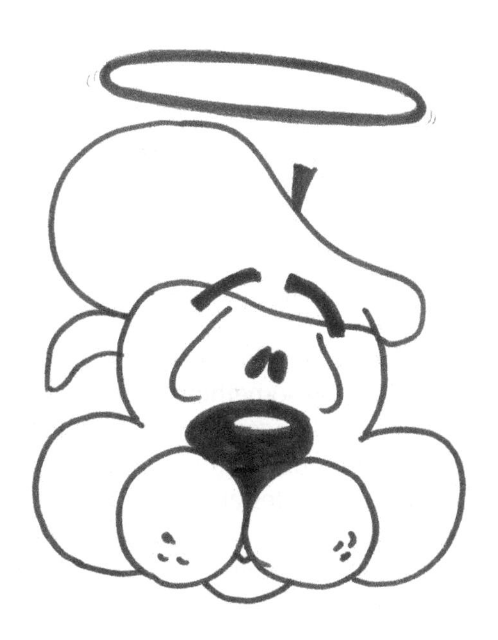

1 An Artist Arrives

As far as I was concerned, my world had begun to turn rather well again. Until the day an Artist arrived at my kitchen door. Now I don't know if you have ever encountered such creatures. Thankfully, sightings are rare. But in my experience, they come from some very alien place indeed.

Imagine my first sight of this particular specimen – slightly disheveled, softly unkempt silver hair (of sufficient length to proclaim 'artist!'), the bright smile of an innocent young puppy, along with an air of being both intimately engaged yet discerningly apart. It was all too clear that The Artist lived by his own rules. Like some wild beast that might, perhaps, be occasionally coaxed but never – never! - commanded. I knew, without question, that this creature would be an unmitigated handful.

Unexpected in his arrival, yet instantly recognised for his significance at this point in my life. Though I was blissfully unaware, as yet, of the imminent chaos his presence could bring. Or of his (for me at least) challenging take on life, which is sure to filter through in subsequent writing. Thus, a very different chapter began.

Food has always been a sensual joy for me. Cooking it, experimenting and letting something new emerge intuitively from the tastes, feel and images in my mind's eye. This has long been an important outlook for my creativity. I have enjoyed a wide range of tastes and foods, from the simple to the sumptuous. In my time, I have been a meat eater, vegetarian and even largely vegan / macrobiotic. And back.

But The Artist was uncompromisingly vegan. Forty years! Passionate about animals and their welfare! Clearly, no shifting this one, then. Indeed, with each visit, I got The Lecture. Gentle, sure. Subtle, yes. But I could see the finger wagging all the same. And, as he pointed out (with just the slightest hint of the finality that comes from a sense of being right), since he possessed all the ethical trumps, there was no valid argument I could muster.

Any sane person would by now have decided that such complexity on two legs would not make for an easy life. And they would be right. So take heed, should your life ever be invaded by an Artist. Run! Take flight! Trust to your instincts. Do not be charmed.

And, naturally, the time came when food was needed, to punctuate and sustain the creative diversions. The Artist and his dog sat near me, hunger burned into their blue (and, respectively, brown) eyes. Each pair pleading 'feed me!' as if they had been eternally starved. I truly did not know which one was the more practised.

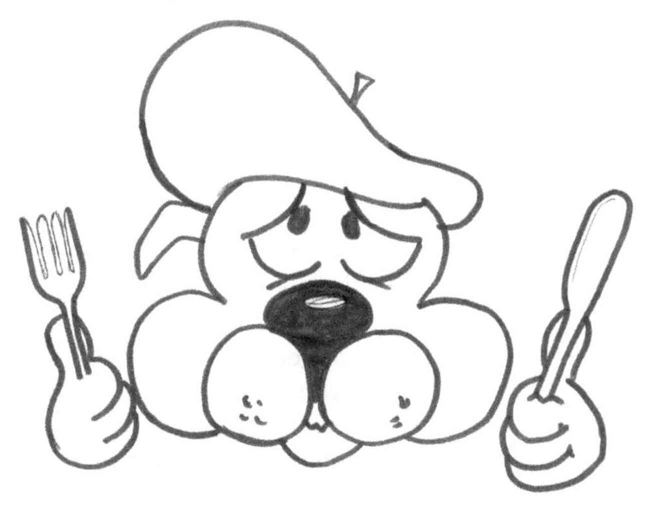

Pleading 'feed me!' as if he had been eternally starved

2 The Feeding of the Artist

And so it started. The feeding of The Artist. (And his dog). Vegan, then, it had to be... So no easy reliance on my delight in artisan butter or delicious cheeses to provide taste and richness.

At a stroke, The Artist had already curtailed my world. And set the norm for how it needed to be. His ethic cast a veto on so many of my regular indulgences. Which meant I needed to adapt. (Though not without offering some challenges to this rather one-sided situation, no matter how thoughtfully considered… of which more later, no doubt).

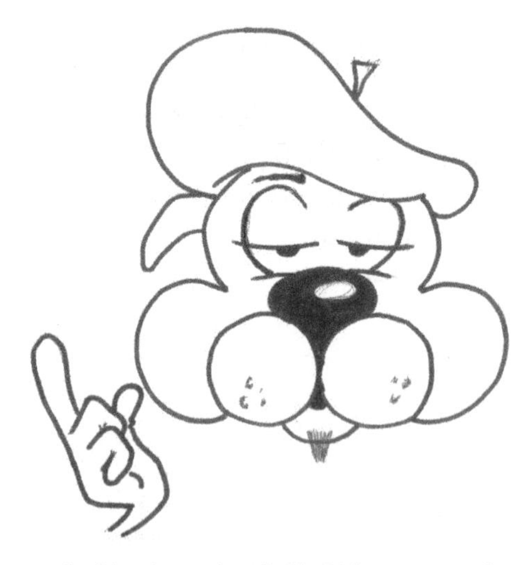

I'd often turn to find he'd wandered off. Oblivious. Mind on higher things

In addition to his vegan intransigence, The Artist was sensitive to wheat, too. Which meant when cooking for him, I needed to avoid all manner of common delights – not only cheese, dairy, eggs, but also wheat, bulgar, couscous, regular pasta, pastry and bread. Handful? The demands this creature set me were so challenging that I began briefly to view him as a prima donna.

Yet I didn't intend to sacrifice my gastronomic standards or taste buds just because The Artist had principles. Looking around, I soon found that there are plenty of recipes for vegans or ideas for avoiding wheat. Few covered both. And too many were hellishly dull. The prospect of endless bland and indeterminate meals paraded in front of my eyes. But no! The cultivation and sustenance of Art is not worth that kind of sacrifice. No matter how good the work is.

Undaunted I embraced my intellectual and creative challenge: to conjure fresh, tasty and interesting things to eat. Meals that pleased me, above all. And hopefully, dishes that would even delight that uber-discriminating creature.

My first offering was Stuffed Peppers.

The soft richness of the peppers filled with onions, celery, carrot, all glistening in fragrant olive oil. My secret additions, including sun dried tomatoes and lemon zest, added considerable flavour and depth. The Artist ate it all. Then, not sure what might be allowed, he wistfully eyed the juices left on his plate, clearly wanting to lick the platter clean. But, that day, he deferred that pleasure to his dog.

Lunch became an almost daily routine. However it always seemed to be me who was cooking it. And clearing it away. And shopping for its ingredients. When called to assist with some minor preparatory task somehow The Artist's creative (butterfly!) mind would turn to musing on some artistic matter, or recalling a forgotten musical track from his early years, that he simply had to google there and then. And I'd often turn to find he'd wandered off. Oblivious. Mind on higher things.

So I would cook. And – oh, is he round for lunch again?

3 'I'll just have a little snack.'

'You should do a book,' The Artist pronounced one day after a particularly satisfying meal.

I considered the suggestion. 'Well, yes. A vegan cookbook. I guess I could.'

' You should. You could call it 'Entertaining an Artist'. With this, he sat back, in smug contemplation. Which it seemed to me was likely to be an end to his contribution to the task.

I cooked. He ate. His dog, being vegetarian from an early age, got the remains that I would otherwise had saved for my supper. I shopped. I cleared away. He googled old clips on You Tube. Well, he was an Artist, after all. And being immersed in something creative (even if it were enjoying a comedy sketch from the 70s) was surely the thing to do. Mundane dealings often seemed, sadly, all too likely to escape notice.

For the most part, The Artist was content to be fed, with little apparent concern about what might appear. So long as something did appear. Occasionally a few scant words of particular appreciation might escape into the ether.

Except for his regular pleas for something sweet to eat.

On each visit, his head would peer around the front door, even before the rest of his body had entered, still stamping his perennially muddy boots on the outside mat. Eyebrows raised optimistically, beaming brightly in an attempt to disarm any possible threat of refusal, I would hear his hopeful refrain. 'Can I have a little snack?'

One might think The Artist had travelled some distance, or undergone some real physical exertion. Instead, it was just fifteen minutes by car. Cue sounds of rice cakes being noisily smeared with peanut butter. It didn't take many days before he found the jam, completing his treat with a sugary topping.

Before many weeks had passed, the accelerated demise of rice cakes, peanut butter, tahini and jam – snaffled on a thrice-daily basis from my cupboards, accompanied by his familiar call of 'I'm just going to have a little snack...,' soon saw me in search of bulk supplies.

A few months later, I showed The Artist the photos I had taken at our first local exhibition of his art photographs. He pouted, 'Do you think I've got a bit of a tum in this photo?'

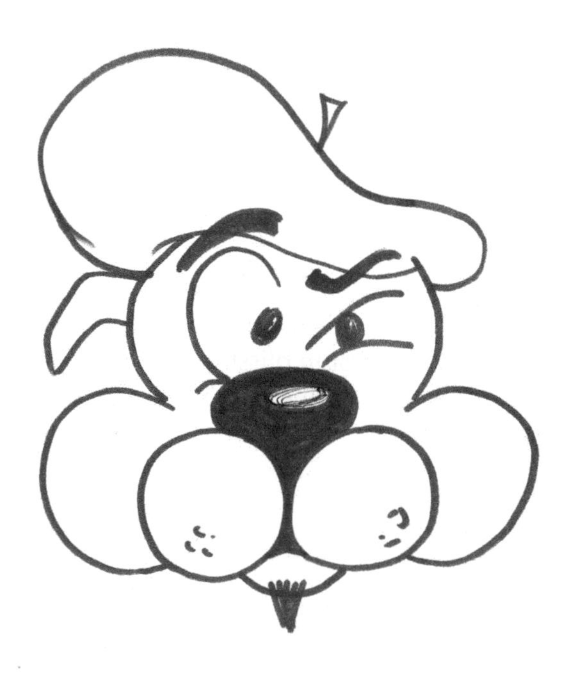

Eyebrows raised optimistically, I would hear his hopeful refrain.
"Can I have a little snack?"

I looked to where he was pointing.

'Or am I leaning so far back in Artistic Contemplation, that my Artist's Scarf has got some kind of a kink in it?'

I prodded said tum. The firmness that greeted my finger made it quite clear that this was not scarf related.

One of the first puddings I created for this insatiable gullet was Aromatic Pineapple, which boasted some unusual ingredients for a sweet dish. I'd found a rather tasty recipe for baked pineapple. But I was lacking most of the ingredients, bar the pineapple itself. No problem, I thought to myself. I'll improvise on the theme.

Steeping it in vodka wasn't too much of a stretch, though I would have preferred something less slavic, such as rum. The vanilla pod added a dusky warmth, though. But it was the addition of fresh mint, perhaps an exotic ingredient for a pud, that truly brought the dish alive. After baking, the concoction tasted satisfyingly sweet yet possessed a pleasing zing. Some soya yoghurt for that essential creamy counterpoint, and it was complete.

The Artist swiftly cleared his bowl, and sat back with a smile across his face, clearly lost in blissful contemplation. One might almost think that craving for something sweet had finally been satisfied.

4 Some Paintings Arrive

One of the delights of adopting an Artist is the inspiration of seeing his art. It started with the canvasses.

Being An Artist, his lodgings were awash with his work, much like ordinary people might accumulate piles of books. He soon brought some canvasses for me to see. This could have been awkward. What if they failed to move me? Or if I thought them unaccomplished? Fortunately, and to our mutual delight, I was thrilled. The Artist was pleased.

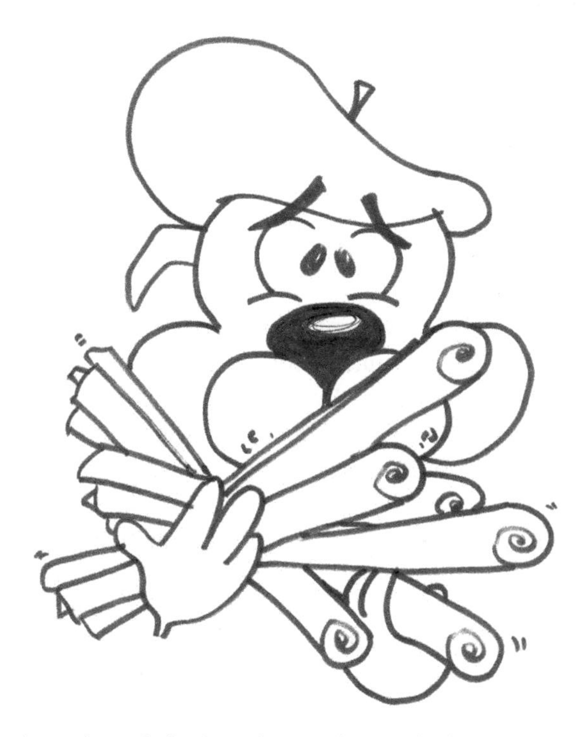

He burst through the front door to deposit the latest armful of art (plus dog) in the hall

The next day, he brought more. We gently unrolled them, whilst he talked about the inspirations that led to their creation. Time passed unnoticed as I was held in rapt attention.

With each day, another armful would appear. The Artist clearly valued his appreciative audience, and I, our conversations traversing a range of artistic matters. But having arrived, and been quietly presented to me, somehow no painting ever left.

Before too long, my living room floor became a repository for The Artist's rolled canvasses. He invited me to hang some so they could be appreciated over time. I improvised by suspending them from a hanger, over a door. Every few days, I found a new delight from the pile – and by now it truly was a pile - to display.

Had it been any other object, the amassed collection that claimed an increasing area of my living room floor might soon have been considered clutter. But this was Art. So I felt privileged to be favoured with its presence.

When visitors arrived, we arranged ourselves around the growing art mountain, quite without complaint. Little did I realise that with this Artist I was harbouring a cuckoo in my nest, who would inexorably take up every last corner of my house, given the chance.

My days soon developed a new rhythm. Swiftly preparing something for our lunch before starting my morning's work, then listening around noon for the familiar sounds heralding The Artist's arrival. I might hear his voice, from a distance, as he gently encouraged his dog along the alley. When he neared, the tramp of his boots. Followed by the whirlwind as he burst through the front door to deposit the latest armful of art (plus dog) in the hall. And often returning immediately to his car, "Just a few more to come", for yet another batch.

This almost daily ritual would unfold with little deviation. The excitement of exclaiming over yet more masterpieces (for surely no other word is allowed when there is An Artist in the house), before settling to yet another lunch. Each meal a masterpiece too, might I say, given the restricted constituents allowed by the Artist's dietary regime.

Given that I needed to prepare our food quickly, in the scant time between breakfast and starting work, it became clear to me that short cuts might be required, so long as quality was not compromised.

In the supermarket I had found a jar of Moroccan-style sauce, which (after scrutinising the ingredients for anything dairy or wheat related) inspired me with thoughts of a Moroccan tagine. My starting point was a favourite, aduki beans. I find them gently energising when I am fatigued. Even the cooking water provides a tasty pick-me-up, so I make sure there is plenty left over for me to drink. (And for The Artist who, before too long, was dosed with a small glass whenever he appeared).

The tagine took shape, as butternut squash, coriander, walnuts and chestnuts claimed their place. It was to be an earthy, rich, restorative dish. The Artist paused, transfixed by his very first forkful, quite forgetting that he was in the middle of describing how he Creates.

It was generally through these non-verbal clues (for he rarely said much at all, except about his own art) that I came to know that The Artist was indeed appreciating my own culinary artistry.

5 The Artist Creates.... in the Kitchen

It wasn't till much later, after (to my mind) foolishly relinquishing command of the kitchen one day, that I realised why remaining in charge was so advisable. It's impossible to imagine The Artist's creative (unhinged?) approach to cuisine, unless you have been the victim of it.

Whilst I am generally very tolerant of other people's ways of doing things (how else could I have survived the tornado of The Artist's having punctured my comfortable routines), I am, like so many normal people, needing at least a few anchor points to cling to.

For most of us the world exists – perhaps even belongs – in categories. That way we know where we are. Even with the subtleties of considering the many shades of grey, some things are clearly 'this', others demonstrably 'not'. With such matters settled beyond apparent controversy (as our own particular world view appears to promise) we are freed to divert our attention to broader matters.

The creative mind, in contrast, transcends categories, or finds that they are fluid and negotiable. Even when they're not. When unleashed in my kitchen, under the pretext of providing sustenance for me, The Artist was so clearly pleased with his Creation that he appeared quite oblivious to the trail of destruction that greeted me, after he had left. Every surface – truly! - containing a used implement, an unwashed plate, a pan (casually askew). 'Clean', merrily mixed with 'Soiled'. Food packets adrift from their usual moorings. Spillages. Perishables left (often somewhere unexpected), awaiting my discovery.

It will come as no surprise at all to learn who had to restore calm and order to the room.

Categories, for me at least, represent an emotional shorthand for understanding the world and, thus, imposing an illusion of order onto life. Many have been instilled from my earliest years, and, thus, being entirely beyond doubt, brook no challenge. For example, take breakfast. I find that there are certain items of food which - irrevocably - belong to that category of 'breakfast'. Surely, this is the True Order of things?

The Artist has no such limitations. I still recall that time when I entered my kitchen to find him cheerfully engrossed in his Creation of a stir-fry. It would be true to say that I wished I had not. I looked on, horrified, at what met my eye. It did extreme violence to my sense of order.

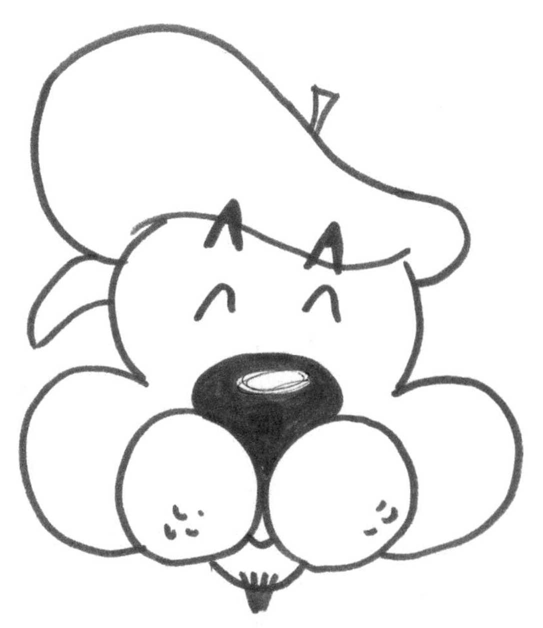

The Artist appeared quite oblivious to the trail of destruction that greeted me

'Is that cooked porridge going in there?' I spluttered.

The Artist looked up, startled out of his creative reverie.

'It was in the fridge,' he nonchalantly replied, clearly puzzled by my query. As if the inclusion was entirely natural.

I retreated, in trepidation of the repast to come. Yet, to my great surprise, when it was presented, our meal looked quite acceptable. And was really rather tasty.

And, would you know it? What I enjoyed the most were those squares of fried porridge, which nestled so neatly, and surprisingly, amongst the vegetables.

The Artist simply smiled, secure in the knowledge that his creative judgement had been proven to be correct. Once Again.

6 More Paintings Arrive

Each day, another painting, or two or three, or more, would appear. My creative appetite was being richly fed with visual treats. But one should always beware of what one wishes for…

Just imagine the scene: my pristine living room, with its gleaming wooden floor, vibrant décor, and carefully placed works of art, a deliberately created calm place for myself, offering a welcome respite and sanctuary from the world.

But no more! Because paintings appeared but somehow never left. Quickly, my living room disappeared beneath wave after wave of Art. My dining table, submerged under The Artist's photography. The floor area shrunk daily under an accumulation of rolled canvasses and stretched paintings. The sofa became shrouded with drafts of The Artist's latest book (to which somehow I had unaccountably become the editor). Meals – once taken in style at the table, then informally on the sofa – were now confined to squatting, bohemian style, on the small area of floor which was, now, the only Art-free zone.

Even a visit to the loo became a hazardous exercise. Canvasses commandeered the floor and laid a trap for the unwary visitor. A couple were stacked by the basin, ready to fall upon the unsuspecting during their ablutions.

'Didn't you hear me say, no more paintings till I've got to grips with what's already here?' I pleaded plaintively.

'No,' The Artist replied, innocently. 'I just keep bringing them because you greet them so enthusiastically. Just love seeing your girlish joy, bouncing up and down in delight at each new painting… So I bring more.'

I could think of no valid argument to his simple acknowledgement of our moments of communion, Artist and Enthusiast, each appreciating and feeling appreciated by the other. I bowed to the inevitable. More Art would surely appear.

During this period of intensive invasion, I acquired several cans of chestnut puree. Both The Artist and I agreed a love of the earthy sweetness contained therein. I was looking for a special sort of inspiration on how best not to squander this precious delight. I was determined not to take the easy route and just do something sweet. Savoury was my quest!

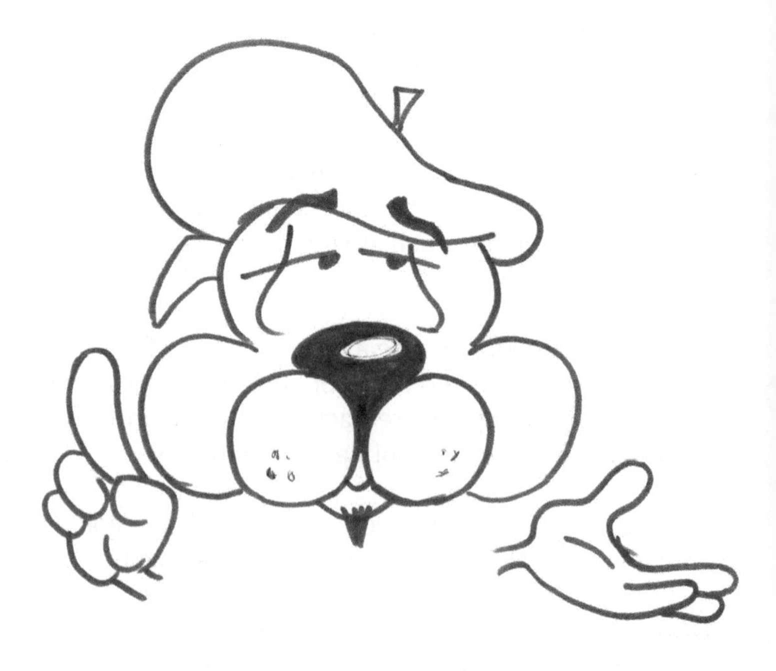

"You greet the paintings so enthusiastically… so I just bring more."

Yet after much research, the most likely starting point I could find was a recipe for a rather dated rice and chestnut bake. It looked like the very worst of 70s wholefood cuisine – stodgy, uninspiring, worthy. But, as I danced carefully around The Artist's stretched canvases face down on the kitchen floor (lovingly steeped in water to tighten them), it soon evolved into something much more interesting.

Given the 70s nature of my inspiration, the brown rice will be no surprise. The chestnut puree, clearly, my star ingredient. I soon realised that their low notes needed the counterpoint of the freshness of sage, lime juice and lemon zest. But the dish did not yet feel complete.

I cast around in my mind, trying out (in my imagination) the tastes and feel of the ingredients I had to hand against the mixture as it currently stood. Seeking that distinctive feeling I get when there is a synchronous match. This is my creative process. The answer – which The Artist, when consulted, arrived at just a few moments after myself - was vegan pesto, to add a richness in the mid-range. It was now complete!

Baked in a loaf tin, the finished dish put me in mind of the sumptuousness of a risotto. Despite no butter or parmesan.

The Artist ate silently, then expressed his appreciation. An infrequent moment. I basked in the rare compliment.

'You see,' he smiled. Smugly. 'I was right. About the pesto.'

7 Of cold weather and hot drinks

An artist can be the most contrary of creatures.

One would imagine that they would be, if nothing else, sharp eyed, noticing every detail in the world that surrounded them. However, from my sorry experience with this Artist, it would appear that that facility is often most selective.

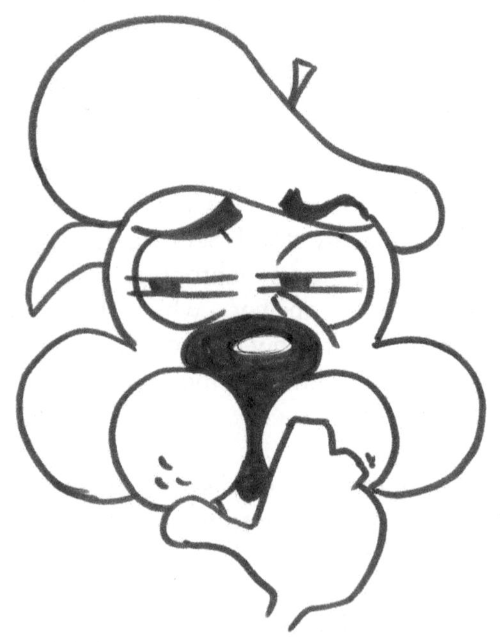

He paused, looking pensive. Something important was clearly about to be emitted

When walking his dog in the woods, a regular ritual, we often stopped to comment on some vista or feature that had caught The Artist's Eye (or, indeed, even my eye, since occasionally it was conceded that perhaps I was learning how to Look).

On this occasion, The Artist made to brush something from my hair. Then stopped and drew back. 'Careful,' he said. 'Your glasses are on your head – I nearly knocked them off.'

'But they're always on my head,' I said. 'That's where I keep them.' He must have seen them there for at least six months. I had to smile to myself, but with the utmost discretion.

It was a cold day and once home, I headed straight for the kettle. On our first meeting, The Artist had stated categorically that he did not drink hot drinks. But with the change in the weather, he had suddenly (without any sense of conscious contradiction) plaintively asked for something to warm the chill. Once again demonstrating that such creatures can be maddeningly arbitrary, with no awareness of being so.

Ever accommodating, I invented something on the spot. Hot soya milk, with two types of sugar (one for sweetness, the other for flavour), real vanilla essence and lime zest. As a source of comfort, it immediately became a popular and consistent request when 'a little something' was in order.

But if you're a tea drinker, like me, then seeking a vegan alternative can be a surprising cause of uncertainty. For the British, one's cuppa is sacrosanct (we all know what we like, because that's what we grew up with, and changes to the formula simply don't taste right).

How to make the transition to a non-dairy cuppa seldom seems to be mentioned in vegan books. Milk is needed to buffer the tannic abrasiveness of tea. But new adopters of this way of eating are left to figure it out themselves, even though it is these overlooked details that show how the whole lifestyle fits together.

In one of those rare moments that his thoughts were not

embroiled in some form of Creative Project, The Artist, who drank neither tea nor coffee, declared himself unable to pronounce on this matter. So I too gave it no further thought.

Later, on a day when I had used the last of the milk in the fridge, The Artist gently nudged me to think about it again. 'Do you really need to buy cow's milk?' he queried. 'You already have plenty of soya milk.'

This was true. I had plenty put by for his warming 'little somethings'. But no matter how masterful was his Art, on no account was I was about to consign myself to the wearisome experience of foul-tasting tea.

I find soya milk too strong-tasting when not incorporated with other tastes. Plus, in my experience, it has often appeared to curdle in hot liquids. To me, this was not visually enticing, nor was it acceptable to my taste.

Neither did going without milk appeal. Black tea, if strong, I find undrinkable. And if weak, not worth the effort at all.

So what to use as a substitute? Rice milk was a possibility. But I found it too thin, too much like skimmed milk. It seemed to bring an unwelcome coolness to the experience. Then the penny dropped. The obvious answer was oat milk. I already knew I liked its warm, sunny and rich flavour.

And, indeed, after just a few days' trial, oat milk did indeed hit the spot. So long as there was a good glug of oat milk in it, my cuppa tasted much like I was used to. Very nice, in fact. But how strange that I could find no easy guidance on this vital matter. Could it be that vegan tea-drinkers around the globe are somehow sworn to secrecy? The Artist pondered this question for all of thirty seconds, before it became eclipsed by a rather more urgent imperative. He paused, looking pensive. Something important was clearly about to be emitted. I waited...

'It's cold,' he pronounced. 'Could I just have a little warm something to drink...?'.

8 Of Sartorial Matters

It would seem that artists have widely varying opinions when it comes to how they present themselves. I am talking here purely in terms of personal appearance. Some clearly pride themselves on natty attire, mixing easily in trendy social circles. Others immerse themselves in their work, happy to hide from any form of limelight in their favourite lived-in splattered garb. Which, of course, immediately identifies them to anyone who comes close enough to observe the splashes.

No need to guess which type of Artist I had adopted. The less elegant, the better, seemed to be his particular sartorial motif.

He arrived one day, clutching some possible publicity photos from earlier years that he wanted to share. I looked at each one, and listened to the stories attached to them. I withheld comment, especially about various hairstyles, which seemed to have their genesis in the 70s. At least the current mane was passable.

However, The Artist's clothes now seemed the same as those he favoured in his youth. Come to think of it, they might even BE the same clothes! I offered to do some washing and chuckled to myself as I anticipated the moment he next encountered his only pair of jeans. It was likely to be with no small degree of shock, as I had ironed them instead of leaving them au naturel, straight from the wash. I wondered if he would know quite what to do with himself, having this semblance of order covertly imposed.

In an attempt to reinstate something of my former life B.A.

(Before Artist), I reminded The Artist, more in hope than anticipation of any success in the matter, that I did have a smart side to my life, which was a necessity for the presentation of said artist to a wider audience. And this transcended the mud-spattered jeans and walking boots made necessary by accompanying said Artist and dog on walks in the wood. Ever quick to turn an unwelcome situation to his way of thinking, The Artist blithely told me he was quite happy for that side of my life to remain a secret to him. In my heart, I knew that this creature was likely to be beyond redemption. But the challenge piqued my interest...

The Artist had made the mistake of showing me a photo from his past in black tie get-up for some charity bash. So I knew he could find his way to scrub up more presentably when he chose. In fact, he had even said as much to me: 'It has been known. But only in extremis...'

But this Artist's simple wardrobe was in part because his needs in life were truly modest, and he preferred to avoid waste wherever possible. He liked to conserve even his oldest clothes, convinced there must still be a good few months of wear to be gotten from them. In the same way, he abhorred wasting the smallest scrap of food.

One lunch time, I had decided to take The Artist's creatively chaotic kitchen routines in hand. I was witness to this 'waste not want not' philosophy in action. Vegetables remained unpeeled and bruised parts were treated with the same esteem as good. Whilst I prepared the butternut squash, onion and peppers for what The Artist had named the Enough! stir fry (in the spirit of Ghandhi's stand on the matter - 'Earth provides enough for every man's need but not for every man's greed').

I imparted a swift lecture on the value of allowing some obviously inedible parts to be wasted. The Artist simply smiled benignly and said they added to the texture. He was comfortable that all the ethical cards were in his hand. I saw from the corner of my eye whole spring onions, roots and outer part not removed, join the rest of the dish.

And I was not swift enough to prevent the broccoli stalk – the woody part – from being incorporated, too. Thankfully, the toasted sesame seeds distracted my attention sufficiently in the finished dish, which, surprisingly, tasted rather well. As always...

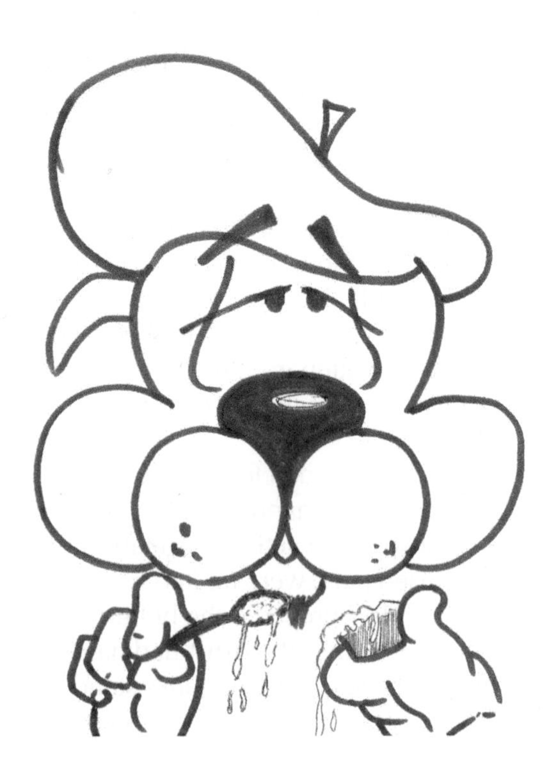

The Artist simply smiled benignly and said the inedible bits added to the texture

9 An Artist's appreciation. And its consequences.

It was a cold day. Yet the light had the promise of spring. I was in the mood for something substantial, comforting and warming inspired by memories of a substantial cassoulet I had enjoyed some years back. A vegan version of this classic French dish sprang to mind, with tofu, tempeh and haricot beans topped by a bubbling, baked crust of fresh breadcrumbs oozing with the cooking juices. The depth and richness of flavour and texture that I recalled in this moment brought a deep smile.

But cassoulet felt too demanding of my time and attention to attempt today. So I quietly gathered from the fridge and let myself discover what wanted to build from this newly remembered taste.

Tempeh is a delight to me, when cooked with understanding. A traditional food originating from Indonesia (and to be found in the freezer section of good wholefood stores), the slab of cooked and fermented soybeans offers a deeply satisfying base note for a meal. I had some ready defrosted, having realised that I needed my tempeh 'hit' once more.

Shooing The Artist out of the way so that I could immerse myself in my creative art (that of devising the dish), I perused the results of my scavenge of fridge and cupboard.

In the background, I could already hear the strains of some googled You Tube clip, followed by the cheers of a football crowd. The Artist had clearly lost no time in commandeering my laptop for what he termed 'a little treat', loving to punctuate his creative day by revisiting comedy clips and music tracks that held delight for him. And following Man City, which he claims is a sensual experience for the true connoisseur. Amongst whose number I clearly am not and, frankly, never wish to be. At least I was spared that experience on this occasion.

I began to sauté some vegetables: my favoured trio of onion, carrot and celery to form an aromatic core of the dish, joined by the sweetness of butternut squash and parsnips. Cubes of tempeh and cooked haricot beans completed the array.

Striving to recreate the depth of taste I was remembering, whilst also incorporating something of the spring feel to the day, the sauce that would integrate the individual components into something of note began to take shape. Tomatoes, intensified by sun dried tomatoes and tamari, were enlivened by lime juice and orange zest. Some fresh herbs and the dish was then ready to bake, as this form of cooking would deliver an extra richness to the repast.

I served it with plainly boiled potatoes which soaked up the sauce. The Artist demolished his plateful rapaciously, his eyes alight with apparent rapture. He immediately had a second portion, of which every last mouthful disappeared with ease.

When he was sated enough to return his attention to me, The Artist told me of the memories my meal had evoked for him. But to my surprise, it was not the tempeh casserole that I had lovingly created. He had been transported by the potatoes.

'I remember my aunt telling me how as a child all my father needed to sustain himself was a big bowl of potatoes,' he confided. 'I inherited his love for that tuber.'

He continued, still captivated by his experience, 'Lightly boiled potatoes, left to absorb whatever sauce has been created within the main dish, are just delightful.'

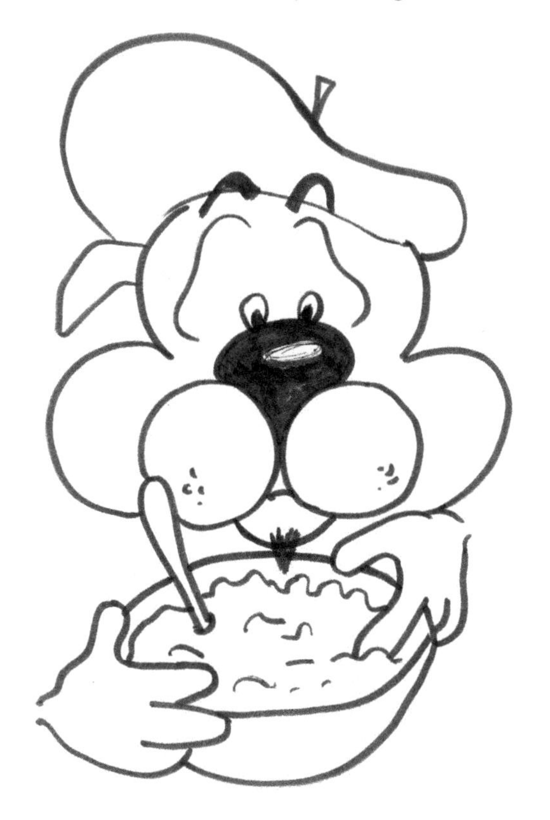

I found him sitting on the stairs, polishing off his third bowl. Which, as it happened, was intended to be my supper

I left The Artist to his musings. But before I knew it, I found him, sitting on the stairs, polishing off his third bowl. Which, as it happened, was intended to be my supper for that evening. He showed no signs of remorse whatsoever.

Later that day, I overheard The Artist talking on the phone.

'I have to say that I could not resist,' he said with some glee, 'but sit on the stairs next to my paintings and finish off the whole dish. Every last scrap. Much to Jacky's chagrin, because rather than recognising how much her efforts were appreciated, she had expected to be able to have some for her supper. Foolish girl!'

Such is the way, it would seem, when consorting with Artists.

Beware!

10 Of artistic vision and digestive concern

I had, by now, become used to The Artist's idiosyncratic style of cooking. I was quite able to chuckle at the latest unusual ingredient discovered mid-mouthful. Left-over porridge had become de rigeur as his signature, but it was invariably surprisingly tasty.

'You'll never guess what's in this one,' he would say, quite enjoying exploiting his reputation for culinary eccentricity to its fullest extent.

And often I could only detect the unexpected ingredient of the day after it had been divulged to me, clearly displaying both pride in his inventiveness and excitement at my anticipated appreciation.

Thus it was that I soon became quite relaxed about the appearance of dates in a savoury dish, or when the remains of the can of baked beans ('it was in the fridge...') added an extra nuance. The Artist was especially pleased when both fried porridge and baked beans were able to be included in the same repast. He felt it rather encapsulated his style.

Should you be in any doubt, his cooking did, somehow, taste rather good. Though on one occasion I did venture to offer a suggestion for minor improvements to the creation. For even I, at my most tolerant, found it a struggle to face no less than six sun-dried tomatoes, left whole, in my bowl.

But I had to recognize that The Artist's creative vision was as fully employed in his cooking as his painting, and thus brooked no correction. Though invariably – as with his art – he offered a new perspective on the experience.

‘I really like the intensity of taste in sun-drieds left whole,’ he explained, responding to the temerity of my opinion. And, having thought about it in this way (whilst personally I would not have risked this degree of intensity), I could appreciate the verve embodied in the choice he had made.

This understanding transferred itself to my perception of his painting. I was about to have the opportunity to appreciate afresh the verve and confidence his work displayed. I had invited a mural painter friend and her partner to lunch, knowing that conversation with a fellow artist was always a delight.

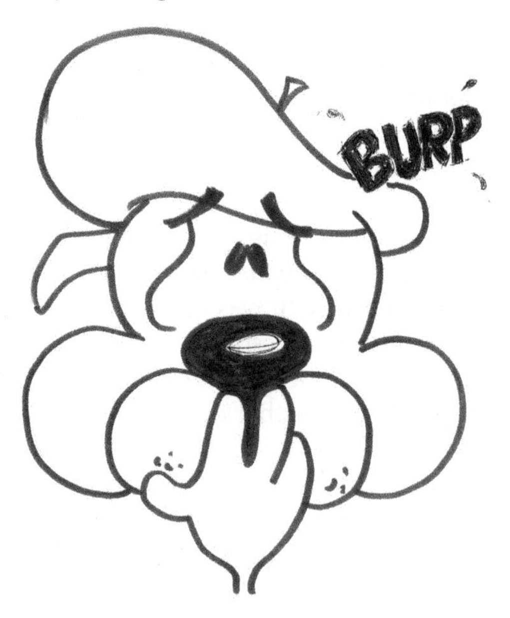

Exploiting his reputation for culinary eccentricity to its fullest extent

And so it proved. After lunch, we browsed through the (now rather large and ever burgeoning) collection of his paintings stacked in my living room. Some of these had migrated to the stairs. And from the stairs to the landing. And, most recently, even to my small bedroom.

He and she lingered in painterly talk, appreciating each other's vision. Though I had to hide a smile when The Artist was questioned on his view about the necessity of symmetry when hanging curtains. He looked quite bemused, since such things did not enter his consciousness. Disorder was the order of his life.

The high point of the day arrived. The painter had brought ladders that could handle the complications of stairs. My intention was to dedicate the stairwell as a private gallery in which to show The Artist's work in its full glory.

The painter's partner was swiftly despatched to climb the ladder and wield the hammer, whilst the artists advised on just where the hangings needed to be placed. Approximately.

I was allowed, however, to choose which paintings from the amassed works were to be given pride of place. Before long, six of his larger works graced the upper reaches of my stairs for my private delectation and delight.

I have been intrigued to witness the transformation that occurs when a finished canvas is mounted on stretchers into its final displayed form. What had appeared good, when flat yet rumpled, took on a certain majesty when stretched. A similar transformation occurs, I could now see, when a painting is moved from floor to wall, to be viewed as the artist had intended.

I said as much to The Artist, in appreciation of his work.

'Don't you wish you had more walls?' was all he had to say.

11 Of the need for 'a little sweetness'

I have always loved art, and have on occasion attended viewings at artists' studios. But having An Artist closely in tow showed me how uncomfortable this calling can be. And therefore why this particular Artist might be in need of so many 'little somethings' to sweeten his day.

Not long after we had first met, he had explained, 'I see my role as An Artist as being to dive deep within myself, examine what is there, and bring it - in an interpreted form - into view for others.'

I thought about this, and tried to imagine what it might feel like. To have one's intimate depths exposed for public view and casual comment. Or worse, perhaps, no comment at all. A scenario bound to revive any anxieties about being liked or approved, should they exist. The Artist explained that for him an occasional 'little something' in the way of a sweet food helped to counterbalance this effect.

****

I was reminded of this when The Artist arrived a few days ago, for an early – 7am! – start to our day. 'Have you got any porridge made?' he breezily enquired as he came through the door. I had, and filled a bowl for each of us.

We ate in silence for a few moments. Until I noticed him peering at his bowl in some consternation. 'There's no raisins in mine!' he exclaimed. 'They're all in yours!'

It was indeed true. They had clumped in the pan. And when

I entered the kitchen a few minutes later, I found him – spoon in hand – hunched over the porridge pot, surreptitiously transferring all the raisins to his bowl. He did not look at all guilty to be caught, mid-raid.

And only yesterday I had witnessed The Artist help himself after lunch to his favourite chocolate soya desserts. They had such a deeply satisfying chocolate taste that I knew how moreish they could be.

I was a little bemused just ten minutes later to see a second one in his hand. The Artist had been attempting some administrative task I had insisted on but he was clearly not enjoying it.

Another ten minutes elapsed. I just happened to look up, as he passed by. 'That isn't your third dessert, is it?' I spluttered. Indeed it was. His Artist's soul clearly would much rather have been painting, and needed the balm that only sugar could bring.

But today, The Artist was noticeably subdued. A favourite painting – a large abstract of glorious blues - had been lent for a charitable cause. It was now retrieved, but had clearly been recklessly used whilst on loan. He stood and surveyed the damage for quite some while, in obvious grief.

Making art is – for This Artist - such a personal act of creation that each canvas carries something essential of his being within it. We shared some moments of silent mourning for what had uniquely been lost, which no words could adequately convey.

After an appropriate time I busied myself in the kitchen. I knew precisely what was needed here.

Creating something to fit the mood, I mixed together hazlenuts (left whole for crunch), chopped prunes and chestnut puree. The dark and earthy tones were thus pierced by the bright insistence of the nuts. These were all gently bound by the comforting creaminess of soya yoghurt. A small dash of brandy completed the concoction, for surely this is traditional as a remedy for shock.

The Artist ate in silence, slowly drawing strength from it. 'I don't suppose there's any more?' he asked. And promptly polished off a further two bowls.

A stonkingly decent pud was clearly no redress for the ruined painting. But I have no doubt that it helped to temporarily ease the pain.

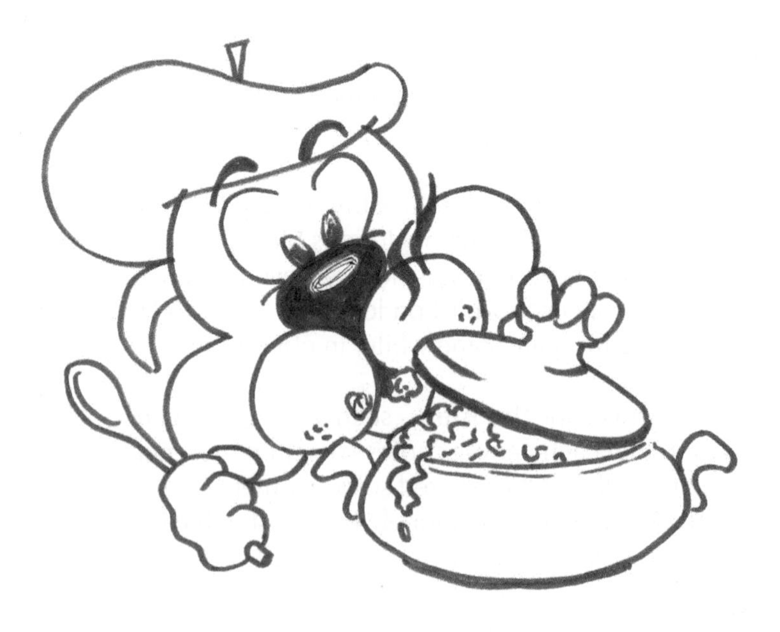

Hunched over the porridge pot - surreptitiously transferring all the raisins to his bowl. He did not look at all guilty

12 Pleasing An Artist

'It really is getting crowded in here' said The Artist, as he surveyed the scant space left in my living room. As if he had just noticed.

'You really are the most patient and tolerant woman I've ever known,' he said solemnly, as I crouched in the only corner of the room currently free of his paintings.

'And not bad as a cook either,' he added cheekily, as if to take attention away from the rare compliment that had just been spoken.

'You know, it's just reminded me of a song. Can we google 'It's Getting Mighty Crowded'?'

And as the notes sung by 60s singer Betty Everett filled the room, I was faced with the sight of An Artist gently wiggling his hips in playful dance, lost in contemplation as he leafed through his paintings and photographs. With an idea in his head, which he had announced as he arrived. 'I've got an idea,' he had cooed. But what that idea was, was yet to be revealed.

The Artist had done the same to me yesterday in his studio. Told me he had an idea but failed to convey what it was. I chose not to intrude into his creative process, knowing that when work was ready for an external eye, it would be presented to me.

But The Artist rang me, later that evening, to ask me what it was he had intended to retrieve from his squirrelled collection of (oh my! could that be yet more?) canvasses.

'I have no idea,' I responded, with an extremity of patience. 'As you haven't yet told me what the idea was.'

'Well if you did know, what might it be?' he asked, in his usual playful yet optimistic fashion, knowing that I would somehow intuitively know.

'Well, you had your idea when you were talking about your key painting for your next exhibition.'

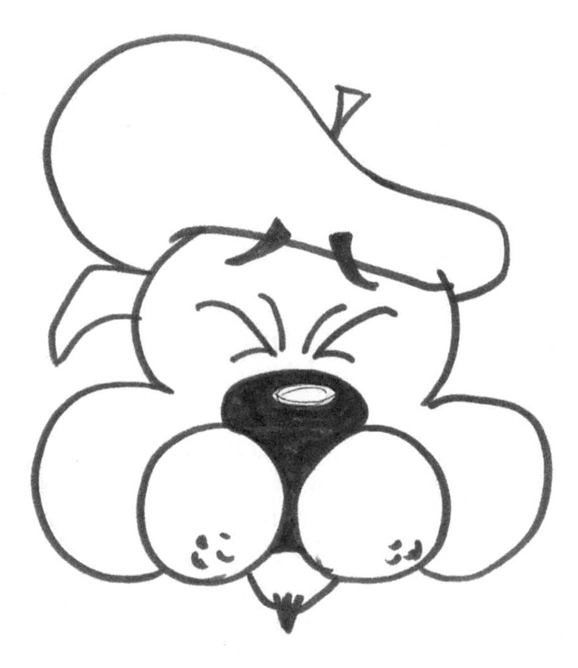

This dish received the most vocal accolade I have ever known escape The Artist's lips

'Ah, of course!' He had remembered. And promptly trotted back upstairs to his store of paintings before he forgot again. Still leaving me in the dark as to quite what his idea might have been.

When next The Artist visited, I had resolved to try a new dish as a treat for him. We'd found a packet mix for idli, a South Indian savoury steamed cake, in the supermarket. It had caught The Artist's eye, and no doubt, appealed greatly to his tummy. But he had soon donated his packet to me, after seeing that the cooking instructions were complicated.

The dish itself was fairly simple. The difficulty was the need for an idli steamer in which to cook the batter - a sort of a circular bun tin that could be immersed in a steamer. I wasn't sure I wished to part with a tenner for one, but I couldn't immediately see how I might construct something similar using my existing kitchen equipment.

Having pondered on it for a few days, the solution had come to me in a flash, as solutions tend to do. I possessed some silicon muffin cases, which would be deep enough (and heat proof enough) for the job. Four would float happily in a pan of water. My makeshift idli steamer was ready.

The rest was surprisingly easy. Making up the rice and lentil batter from the mix took no time at all, saving me the day or more of pounding and fermenting it would have taken to make from scratch. Spooning the mixture into the muffin cases, the idli were ready after 15 minutes of gentle steaming.

To go with them, I made a coriander chutney. The fragrant tang of fresh coriander leaves, blended with coconut, garlic and chilli, was then bound with soya yoghurt. The resulting green paste looked really very tasty indeed.

I served the idlis topped with the coriander chutney. The Artist, his fork already extended in anticipation, took his first bite.

This dish received the most vocal accolade I have ever known escape The Artist's lips. Although it clearly originated much deeper, from the depths of his stomach and from his memory of past travels.

'Mmmm. This is delicious,' he groaned in pleasure.

'It's very good indeed,' he added.

'I really like this,' he said, a few mouthfuls later.

'It's what I had for breakfast when I was in Sri Lanka,' he reminisced. 'Temple breakfast, Tamil style. Now that really set me up for the day.

'With the chillis it felt like I had two brandies in my tummy.'

It was no surprise to me at all that this was soon followed by...

'Is there any more?'

13 In which The Artist seeks a manager

The subject of his need for a manager arose soon after The Artist first crossed my threshold. He was describing how difficult it was to tackle the discipline of business whilst inhabiting an Artist's mindset. The two activities operated from quite different sides of the brain.

The matter raised itself again barely two weeks into our acquaintance. 'I really do need a manager, you know,' was his opening gambit on the matter, as we made our way back from a very damp walk. 'You'd be good at it. You could take on the business side of things,' he continued, rather hopefully. 'Whilst I do the creative bits.'

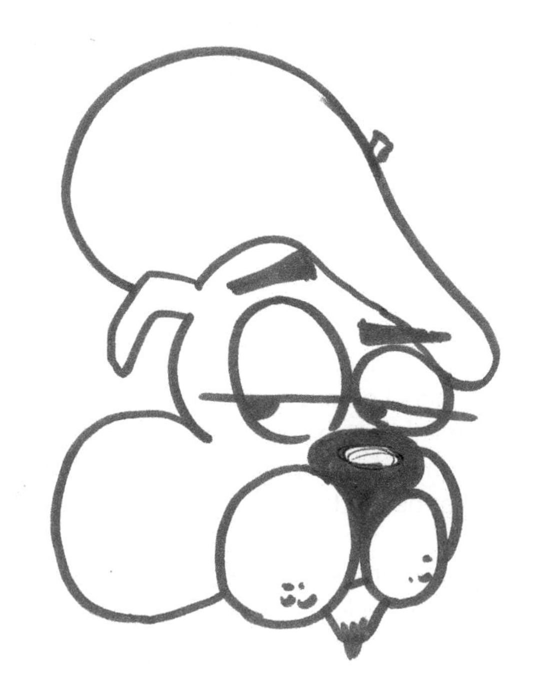

"Would you have a little something sweet by way of pudding?"

I pondered this offer for a few moments, in silence, as we trudged along the riverbank. As it started to rain, I put my jacket on. But he had not thought to bring one. I mused on how this rather summed up the lack of shielding an artist, or at least This Artist, generally carries against the world. And why someone acting as an outer shell is needed to allow an artist to remain open enough to work from a deeper place.

I thought that perhaps I should clarify the terms of this unexpected offer, especially as we had barely just met. I already had quite enough in my life needing my attention as it was. Plus it had immediately struck me that the fun bits did seem to have been rather unequally shared out.

'So,' I asked, 'Are you asking me to throw over the whole of my life, then, in order to manage yours?'

The Artist smiled patiently. 'Well, only some of it,' he said, in all apparent sincerity. 'You could still have one or two days for your own projects,' he said with a smile.

Flattered as I was to be asked, I gently declined the offer. I could already see that managing This Artist was likely to be a gargantuan task.

We returned to my place, chilled from the rain and in need of rapid sustenance. Looking at the contents of my fridge, I pulled out a few things that I knew would be speedy to prepare, and in my mind began to concoct simple ways in which they might be made satisfying to eat.

First, one of my favourites: pan-fried tofu. Perfect for when something quick is needed. Indeed I sometimes think of it as the closest vegan alternative to fish fingers. I cut the tofu lengthways into slices, patted it dry and rolled it in polenta.

Shallow frying provided a crisp yellow crust with soft, yielding tofu within.

To complement the low-key taste of the tofu, a savoury sauce was indicated. There's nothing simpler than sautéing sliced onions and grated courgette in olive oil till they are soft, then adding tamari (soya sauce made without wheat) to taste.

The repast was completed by small cubes of sweet potato, boiled till soft. The size of the cubes allowed for a shortened cooking time. And finally a salad, to provide freshness. To salad leaves I added grated carrot for sweetness, toasted pumpkin seeds and salad dressing.

Pumpkin seeds are delicious, but enter an entirely new stratosphere of moreishness when dry toasted in a pan till lightly browned and popped, like popcorn. The warmth of the toasted seeds contrasted with the moistness of the vegetables, the crunchiness of the tofu with the softness of the leaves. I casually whizzed these dishes onto the table for our 'Fast as a Flash' lunch.

It was evident that The Artist had been inspecting my DVD collection whilst I cooked. We clearly shared an interest in arthouse films and he had already earmarked dozens - pulling them out a few inches so that he would not forget which they were - that he wanted to watch.

Had I but had the prescience to realise it, this was an early indication of the extent to which my life, house (and belongings) would soon be commandeered in the cause of Art. But at this point I was still blissfully naïve to this fact.

The Artist inspected the dishes I had prepared. He greeted

the taste of each one with an appreciative sound. The pan-fried tofu was new to him. He particularly liked the savoury flavor of the onion with courgette, and closely queried me on how it had been made. He made mention of the pumpkin seeds as being especially pleasing. And the sweet potato disappeared in the same manner as it had been cooked: 'fast as a flash'.

Sated, we rested in our chairs, separately contemplating the warmth in our stomachs and the vibrant tastes lingering in our mouths.

Then...

"That was very nice. Thank you," broke the silence.

The Artist continued, with words to which I was soon to become accustomed. "Would you have a little something sweet by way of pudding?"

14 The Milk of Kindness

My friend surveyed the contents of my fridge door. Quite bemused.

Some people are connoisseurs of wine, and can extol the merits of a Sauvignon or Merlot. Others might be aficionados of cheese, and appreciative of the distinctive qualities of brie, or stilton. Or even simple mousetrap cheddar.

She turned to me, eyebrow raised in question. I could see I would need to explain.

"It's the result of my association with The Artist," I began. "I seem to have become something of a 'plant milk' buff."

Indeed there were no less than five different types in play, in my fridge. Each with different culinary qualities. But I had sampled at least nine in the last few months.

I pointed to the far end of the row of cartons. "This one's soya milk: the best known alternative to cow's milk and, generally, the cheapest, too. I prefer not to use it in tea, though, as it can curdle and I think its taste too intrusive.

"But it is my mainstay when cooking. When I wish to moisten a dense porridge, or to make a white sauce or custard, it is soya milk that I will turn to. It also makes a rather satisfying hot drink, mixed with sugar and vanilla."

My friend - slowly - absorbed that information.

Next to it, I could see the rice milk.

"This is The Artist's favourite," I continued, "especially when combined with vanilla, and he drinks huge quantities of it to quench his thirst."

My friend nodded sagely, clearly glad to be on somewhat lighter ground.

"I find it too 'thin'," I added, "much like semi-skimmed milk, so I tend to leave it exclusively for him.

"I have to say," I confided, "I am, now, quite used to finding empty cartons left haphazardly on my kitchen worktop, awaiting recycling or disposal. And, unfortunately, even more used to finding half-full ones, absentmindedly left out, in danger of going off."

She laughed, recognising the description from her own encounters with The Artist. From the other room we could hear the sounds as he googled the latest football highlights. If his team should have lost, I had no doubt he would soon be in need of a 'little something' to soothe the disappointment.

"This one's almond milk," I warmed to my subject, "but, you know, it's been quite a disappointment. I thought it would taste more strongly of almonds, and had high hopes that it might be suitable for tea. But it curdled badly when added to my brew, and its taste was more subtle than expected."

She shifted her weight. I wasn't sure that my friend had bargained for quite this amount of explanation. But she had asked and I had started and so…

The almond reminded me that my abiding favourite was hazelnut milk, found quite unexpectedly in a downmarket supermarket that I would not have predicted to be alert to the fineries of vegan dining.

The strong, sweet nuttiness of hazel shone through, and was simply delightful in tea. Rather like the shot of flavoured syrup offered in coffee bars, only without the sugary undertones. I could happily have rested with this as my main source of designer milk (coupled with the workhorse of soya for the basics).

I thought I had better not burden my friend with that information too. But as hazel was not always available, I had had to continue my quest for the perfect vegan milk.

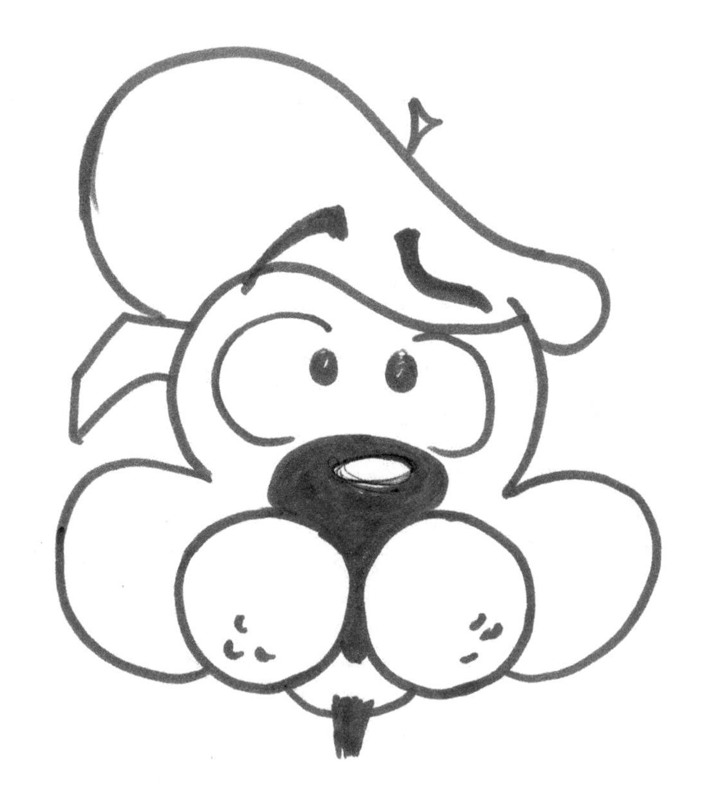

"Did I hear anyone mention dessert?" he smiled hopefully

"Have you tried this one?" I asked, as I picked the carton next to the almond. 'It's hemp milk. More expensive than some, but quite acceptable in tea and, of them all, probably most like cow's milk in taste and texture." I could see this being a regular in my fridge door.

My friend shook her head. "And what's this one?" Her curiosity now engaged, she pointed to the carton jammed in beside the hemp.

"That one's specially treated soya milk, to make it less likely to curdle in tea and coffee."

It certainly achieved this aim. I could imagine its rich taste being particularly satisfying in coffee, in place of cream. I could also see that this might recommend its use in a creamy dessert of some kind.

In my mind, I immediately had visions of a certain Artist in considerable bliss, should such a dessert happen to materialise before him. I resolved to try it out, before too long.

This last milk reminded me of a new brand of tea I'd recently noticed in the supermarket. It had been formulated especially so that soya milk would not curdle. Clearly the vegan voice was beginning to be noticed in the mainstream world. Especially with the increasing prevalence of alternatives to avoid allergies.

"My favourites are hazel, and oat milk," I revealed. "Oat feels warm, happy, almost buttery when I drink it, and works well in tea. There seems to be a difference between different makes, though. With some, I have found it is best to shake the carton anew each time, otherwise the best of the liquid sinks to the bottom, leaving just the thin stuff being poured."

My friend pulled out yet another variety she had noticed on the counter. Quinoa milk. Made from the Peruvian grain, so sure to be high in protein.

"This one looks interesting," she exclaimed. I frowned. I hadn't gotten accustomed to its aromatic taste yet, and certainly not in tea.

"It really would not do," I concluded, "to end our tour, without paying due acknowledgement to chocolate flavoured soya milk. A firm favourite of The Artist. There always has to be a few, in this corner of my kitchen. Which has now turned into a vegan milk hoard. Just in case his need for 'a little something' should be chocolate dependant."

My friend smiled. She had heard the tales...

"Though, these days," I mused, "he does seem to have moved on to a serious 'chocolate soya dessert' habit instead. Happily eating two, or three, in quick succession. And, invariably, I'll find the evidence strewn somewhere quite unexpected."

As if on cue, The Artist appeared.

"Did I hear anyone mention dessert?" he smiled hopefully.

15 If Delia can do it...

Even the venerable Delia acknowledges that the busy cook should consider short cuts, having produced a book on how to 'cheat' by using ready-made components. So if Delia could do it, surely lesser mortals are allowed.

Whilst I may have started my vegan adventures full of innocent zeal, cooking from fresh each time, the reality is that there are times when something rapid is essential.

My solution to this has been to use some bought items to speed or simplify the cooking process. But only the very best. Ready-made sauces could be particularly useful, as were gourmet tins of unctuous aubergine baked with tomato and garlic. The Artist's beloved Idli mix (a kind of savoury rice and lentil 'cake'). And puds (for who could spurn An Artist his delight?) might be based around a soya dessert that was his avowed favourite.

Alas, The Artist did not possess sufficient discipline to cook to a deadline, tending instead to become so immersed in his lateral culinary thinking that he lost all sense of time.

One day – timeliness being crucial as I had arranged to meet others – The Artist offered to make lunch. He had intended for it to be a treat. I accepted, but made it clear that we needed to eat in just ten minutes and was very happy for something quite simple to appear.

Half an hour later, aware that something was seriously amiss with the timings, I peered in the kitchen. The Artist was blithely in full Create: stirring, chopping, pondering which improbable ingredient was to be the star discovery today.

'We need to go in fifteen minutes,' I told him, anxiously, my pretend deadline (adopted as a result of my experience of The Artist's rather loose relationship with time) now dead in the water, with the real one approaching its last gasp too. 'This really does need to be ready now'.

I was shooed away, for the dish was not yet matching his vision. And when it arrived, eventually - elaborate, lovingly cooked - we had just five minutes at most to eat. It looked enticing, but I had to leave, unfed.

Had I been allowed to cook, I might have considered a simple stir fry, easily ready in ten minutes. Just a few days back I had sautéed onion, celery, green pepper and broccoli till they were softening, but still retaining their flavours. A quick hit of the exotic (on this occasion a ready-made coconut and chilli marinade) plus a large handful of watercress, rocket and spinach, and the dish was done.

Dessert had been equally rapid – bought chestnut puree given depth by a soya chocolate dessert (always guaranteed to get An Artist's approval) then complexity added by chopped prunes, vanilla essence and a swirl of tahini for creaminess. The Artist had quite delighted in it, soon calling for seconds.

Other simple dishes might involve a baked potato, steaming hot from the oven, moistened with olive oil (instead of butter) plus a quick topping. Interesting varieties of hummus worked well in this respect (my favourites being lemon and coriander, or broad bean with mint). And we were pleased to discover that our tins of baked aubergine made for a most satisfying sauce here.

When served with a speedy salad - grated carrot, finely sliced peppers, lemon juice, tomatoes, spring onions and a sprinkling of toasted sunflower seeds, we felt we had dined well with a minimum of fuss.

****

The Artist had been away for the last week, travelling afar to places he had once lived, and where – squirrel like - he still had paintings stored. Yes, yet more of them! He had set off with the promise (or was that the threat?) that some of them would be returning home with him.

To welcome him back (and, given his penchant for my cooking, to give him an olfactory homing beacon), I cooked a 'Welcome Back' repast. We had not spoken yet that day, so he could not know when lunch might appear. Unerringly, he arrived bang on 1pm. How did he time it so well?

He greeted me immediately with a cheery 'Have you built that extension yet?", as he unloaded canvas, after unrolled canvas, after stretched painting, after canvas. My living room floor, only so recently regained, was once more awash with his work. I did, indeed, need extra space to store this quantity of art.

Lunch eaten, I served dessert. A simple concoction, but sophisticated enough for when friends came to eat, too. Chopped dessert apples (which call for less sugar than the cooking variety) had been lightly cooked in a little water with sliced oranges. The zest of the oranges added intensity. Finally, a fragrant, natural, brown sugar brought a certain sweet stickiness to the hot liquid.

After the fruit had softened sufficiently, the whole was allowed to cool and infuse. It was served in small bowls, with the sugar-sweetened zest artfully scattered on top.

The Artist had eaten it, thoughtfully yet most appreciatively.

It was only some weeks later that he made reference to it, asking me to make it again. It was soon clear that he assumed I shared his own experimental approach to food.

'You know,' he said, 'that one with the grated carrot on top.'

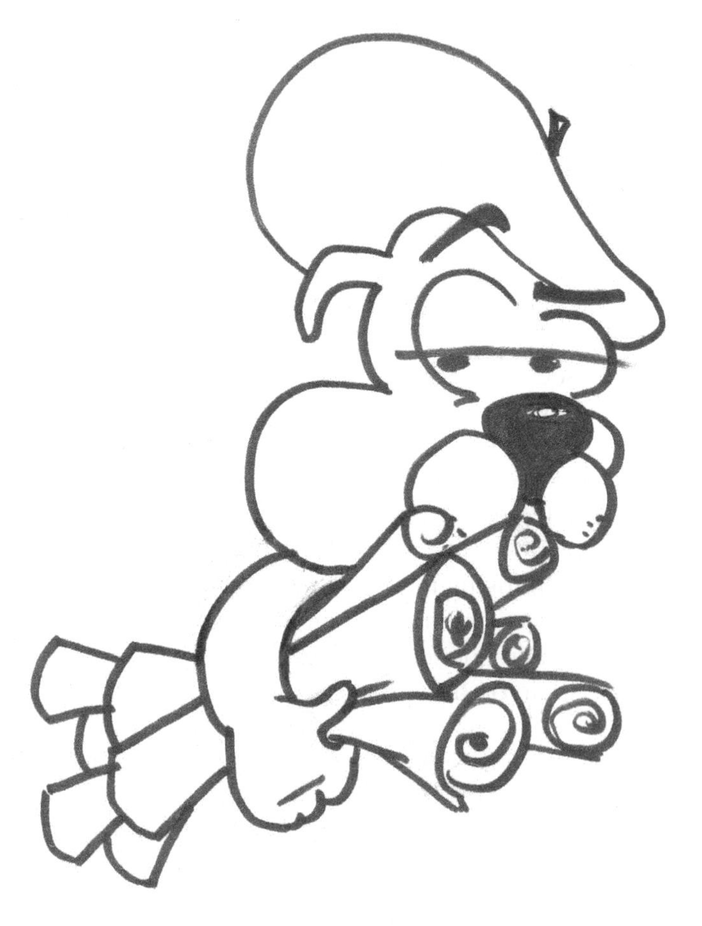

He greeted me immediately with a cheery "Have you built that extension yet?", as he unloaded canvas after canvas

16 On becoming The Artist's manager

There was an inevitability to it. Becoming The Artist's manager.

For quite some months, I had carefully observed the point at which a supportive stance tipped over into taking on some of the tasks that go with earning one's living as An Artist. And had been most careful to keep myself on the non-doing side of that point.

It was not that I did not wish to be of assistance. But I could see the enormity of the task, and instinctively knew that should I ever start to become ensnared in Artistic dealings, that there could be no escape. Plus, no small point: my life was already full enough earning my own living.

But I could see The Artist did need help. I was willing to offer a few days in which to help him identify the different strands to his creative endeavours (there were so many!), so that he could present each part to the world coherently, instead of everything being enthusiastically muddled together.

For The Artist, thinking in this new way brought a peculiar degree of stress, such that our concentration was broken with increasing frequency by his need for 'a little something' to ease the strain on the Artistic brain.

Eventually, we completed the task. Doing this had allowed us to see that The Artist needed at least four separate channels to encompass the range of his work, and to allocate each aspect to its natural home.

We mapped everything that he did into these new categories. The Artist was truly most appreciative. At last, he had a way of talking about his work that would not overwhelm the listener. But he was not yet used to this new way of thinking. And proclaimed in great confusion one day, 'I've been separated into so many bits I don't know which part belongs where!' before heading into the kitchen for a comforting little something.

I had thought I would be safe to offer this simple assistance, without running the risk of taking on the whole of this cause. Alas, I should have heeded my own premonitions.

And so, over the next few weeks, as we continued to instil some order into his working life, I (imperceptibly) became The Artist's manager. And, somehow, by degree, the chaotic vortex that characterised his existence began to infuse mine.

I commented, sadly, that my life would never be the same. The Artist cheerfully agreed, just saying, 'I am as I am'. I knew I would simply have to submit gracefully.

We decided to organise an exhibition of his work. In the carefree days (clearly now forever gone) when I could visit art exhibitions with nothing more on my mind than the promise of visual enjoyment, I had spared no thought as to how the paintings arrived in their temporary lodgings.

I soon discovered just how much work was involved in making it happen. The Artist, somewhat naively, had hoped we could just turn up and somehow organise things on the day. That had been his way. But he had reckoned without his new manager's firm views on presentation.

So we began. Selecting which paintings (or photographs) to

show. Mounting, framing, signing by the artist. Signs, labels, prices. How to hang the art. And on what. Advertising. Printing of flyers. Distributing them. Wrapping and transporting the paintings. Unloading, and creating the f inished exhibition for others' enjoyment. Loading it all back again, and transporting home.

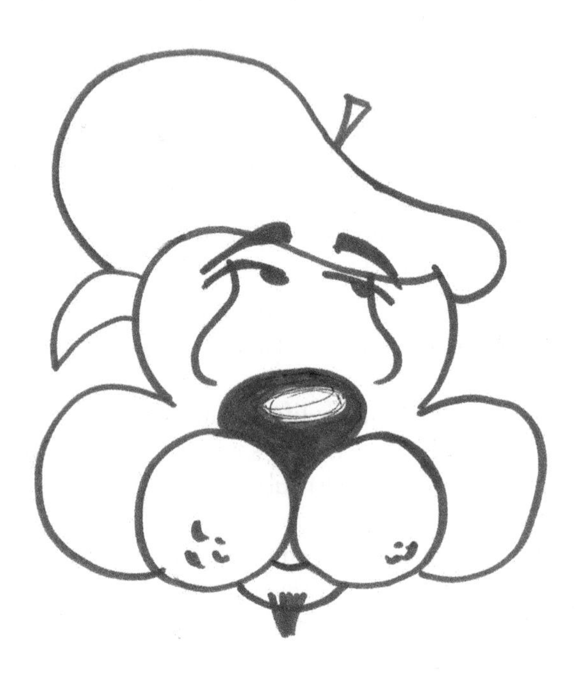

Before long he was humming to himself, quite happy with the world, as he prepared his paintings for exhibiting

The Artist punctuated all of this preparatory work with small diversions of his own to lift his day. He would frequently disappear, only to be found dipping into a newly opened packet of dried fruit. 'I just needed a little something,' he would say. Or watching football highlights:

'Just a few minutes!' he would promise. But before long he was humming to himself, quite happy with the world, as he prepared his paintings for exhibiting.

Gradually, it all got done. We were ready. I surveyed my living room, normally cluttered in every direction with The Artist's work. I blinked.

'I've just seen floor!' I exclaimed. 'Paintings have been moved!' The Artist merely smiled, and said it wouldn't last long, so not to get too excited.

We settled to a well-earned lunch.

Quite my favourite dish is simple pan-fried tempeh (a delicious traditional food made from soya beans), its savoury golden crust accompanied by the sweetness of crisp roast potatoes and the freshness of lightly cooked spring greens, all glistening with plenty of gravy made with tamari (a good quality soya sauce made just with soya beans and no wheat) and the pan-fried juices. The delight contained in each mouthful! I could never tire of this meal.

I asked The Artist his views, hoping he shared my enthusiasm for the tempeh. 'It is certainly an exotic ingredient,' he began, 'with an exceedingly interesting texture. And for which you clearly have a personal passion.'

I waited. The Artist was not sounding quite as enthusiastic as I had hoped. 'It's very tasty indeed,' he continued. 'But I have to declare that I am more enraptured by the roast potatoes. They just happen to be a particular passion.'

There could be no arguing with this.

The rest of the week passed. On the day of the exhibition, at the venue, with barely an hour till opening and plenty yet to be done, I looked around. No Artist!

I searched, eventually finding him outside, captivated by some blossom, taking photos. Quite oblivious to anything else.

It was The Deal. Well, in his mind, at least. The manager made it all happen. He, as Artist, was left free to Create.

I ruefully acknowledged my fate.

17 Of creative rebellion

We were preparing for an important exhibition of The Artist's paintings. Together, we'd chosen more than thirty of his Nudes for display (which in my view were of as good as any of the work of several eminent artists).

The Artist had exhibited many times before, but this was the first time he was going to have to meet my exacting standards. I rather got the impression that there were times when he was quite regretting the imposition of my discipline upon his chaotic preparations.

Many of the paintings needed to be framed or stretched for the exhibition (given his prolific output over the years, there simply wasn't space to store everything in its final form). So we had gotten all the materials together, choosing frames and mounts to complement his paintings. But with the paintings currently in progress, there was no space left in his studio to prepare.

I had little option but to install The Artist in my living room with instructions to apply himself to getting it all ready for showing, with every possible implement he might need made ready and a checklist of how I wanted each one done.

I returned, later that day, to a note, documenting his progress. There was no sign of the Artist though. He had rewarded himself with an early finish. There were however another thirty framed paintings in the room. And no floor space at all, bar a few square feet.

I had designated the next day for cataloguing and labelling the work. One by one, The Artist presented each painting whilst I prompted for details – its title, the medium, the price. His mind constantly wandered to more intriguing matters (and no, I wasn't going to google that song for him just now), whilst I repeatedly called him back to the task.

It was only through the soothing qualities of several 'little somethings' that we managed to complete the task.

Ordeal over, The Artist invited me to inspect the paintings, to make sure I was happy with the standard of presentation. 'Where's your Artist's label?' I soon queried. 'The one that should go on the back, so people know it's a painting by you.'

The Artist pouted, clearly hoping I wouldn't have noticed his deliberate omission. 'I have signed the paintings,' he said, hopefully. 'On the front. Isn't that enough?'

It was not.

With a deep sigh, The Artist yielded to my insistence. Though not without making it clear that he had differing views on the matter. But clearly feeling he had, perhaps, met his match on this occasion.

He began to cut out the labels I had prepared, sticking each one to the back of the frame and annotating them with the name of that painting and the flourish of his signature.

I busied myself in the kitchen, knowing that it was better to leave This Artist feeling that he had some control in his affairs. Our treat today was to be vegan burgers, made from freshly cooked chickpeas.

Chickpeas present something of a cooking marathon, as they

need soaking overnight, then a couple of hours on the stove. For many meals, I find tinned will do just fine, and are decidedly more speedy. But there are times, such as now, when fresh delivers an infinitely better result.

I prefer a bit of texture to my burgers, so only roughly mash the chickpeas, which helps the mixture to cohere but leaves chunks intact. The process can feel quite primeval, as the best method I have found is to pound the beans with the end of my wooden rolling pin. Much like a giant pestle and mortar.

I gently sautéed the ingredients that would add an aromatic dimension to the mix: onion, garlic, chilli. Then added it with the chickpeas, along with lemon zest, fresh coriander, plus tahini and oats to bind.

I shaped it by hand into small burgers, applying pressure to achieve a firm, flattened patty. Then gently (for they need a delicate touch at this point if they are to retain their shape) shallow fried them on each side.

We ate. The Artist made enthusiastic and appreciative sounds with each mouthful. He seemed particularly cheery, clearly very satisfied with his efforts that morning. All appeared well.

But not for long. I soon became aware of a sinking feeling in my belly. Intuitively, I knew that something was amiss.

I checked. The Artist had indeed attended to the majority of his paintings, as instructed. But each label had been cut with wildly varying borders around the text. Some, stuck slightly askew. Or barely stuck at all.

'But I like it this way!' he declaimed.

I sighed, with as much patience as I could summon. 'Next time I think I'd better be in charge of this bit.'

The Artist did not argue the point.

Later, as he was leaving, pausing to lace his boots, he said, 'You see, I can settle down to something. Just so long as you let me have my little moments of rebellion, now and then.'

'Little moments?' I laughed. 'Every single painting now carries, on its reverse, a very visual indication of your rebellion today.'

The Artist brightened, clearly delighted that his refusal to conform was now so indelibly preserved.

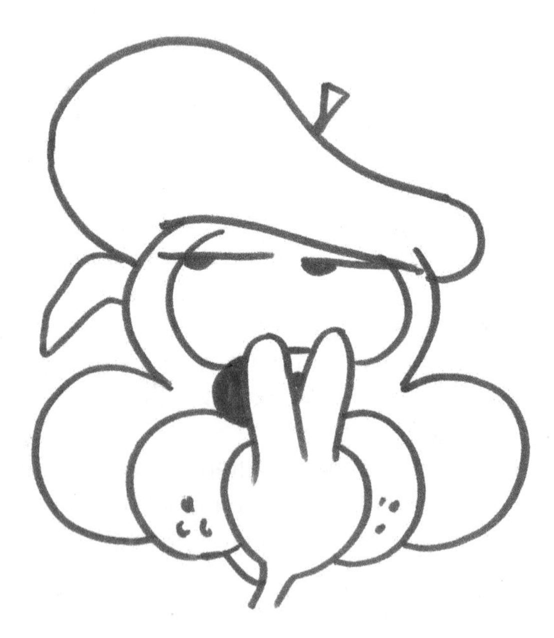

The Artist brightened, clearly delighted that his refusal to conform was now so indelibly preserved

18 On managing An Artist (and one's life...)

When An Artist invades one's life, then art – looking at it, talking about it, seeing moments that could inspire art, being surrounded by canvasses, dealing with the pragmatics of presenting that art to the world - becomes a daily happening.

I had, by now, accustomed myself to the ebb and flow of floor space in my living room as paintings arrived, left, were rearranged, and (seemingly) multiplied overnight. And to the not-so-gradual appropriation of the rest of my house by canvasses, stretched paintings and framed work.

Periodically The Artist would arrive, glance around as if seeing the clutter (if items of sensual delight could be termed so) that he had caused. Occasionally he would comment, as if he had just that moment realised, how untidy my home had become. Or, playfully, that I really should get a bigger house. To contain more of his paintings, of course. I never did detect any signs of remorse.

It was surely only inevitable that the influx would continue.

'Morning!' he cooed, his beguiling, ever hopeful smile to the fore, as he arrived with yet another armful of rolled canvasses.

'I was wondering,' he continued, 'what your loft is like. Is it boarded?'

Thus it was, that the final free space in my house was casually commandeered.

Even my garden had been territorially marked. It would at

times be pressed into use, on fine days, for preparing artwork for display. The light was stronger, so the work could be seen more clearly. And it was perfect for any water splashes from sponge-cleaning, and tightening the stretch of each canvas through soaking.

I enjoyed seeing The Artist outside, attending to his paintings. Humming softly to himself, lost in his own thoughts, happy to be immersed in art-related tasks. It was quite a treat to see the finished array of work, left to dry in the shade. Colourful, like so many exotic flowers.

The garden came into its own as a photo studio too. When we needed to photograph the larger canvasses, outdoors was the only space big enough. Paintings laid out on the paving, whilst The Artist nimbly hopped onto my garden table to gain sufficient height to capture the whole.

The canvasses seemed to get bigger, as time went on. Visiting friends would be pressed into holding them aloft, so that a good likeness could be taken.

'Now, this next one's eighteen feet long,' The Artist said, in all seriousness. 'You'll have to hold it up high, so I can get it all in.'

Our arms, at their fullest stretch, were not sufficient. This one insisted on sagging in the middle. Two people, one at each end, would simply not do. I thought quickly, and ran next door to enlist the neighbour.

What fun - the three of us, arms at full tilt, trying to stay hidden behind the canvas whilst keeping it taut. The Artist directing us for the shoot. Me, perched on a chair (being shorter than the other two, my end of the canvas needed a helping hand on the height). Only noticing – too late – that the arm of the chair had made it into the bottom edge of the picture.

And afterwards, reclaiming the table and sharing a summery warm pasta salad together. Good quality gluten free pasta, glistening in the sun from its coating of fragrant olive oil, and laced through with the unctuousness of soft-braised onions, celery and pepper.

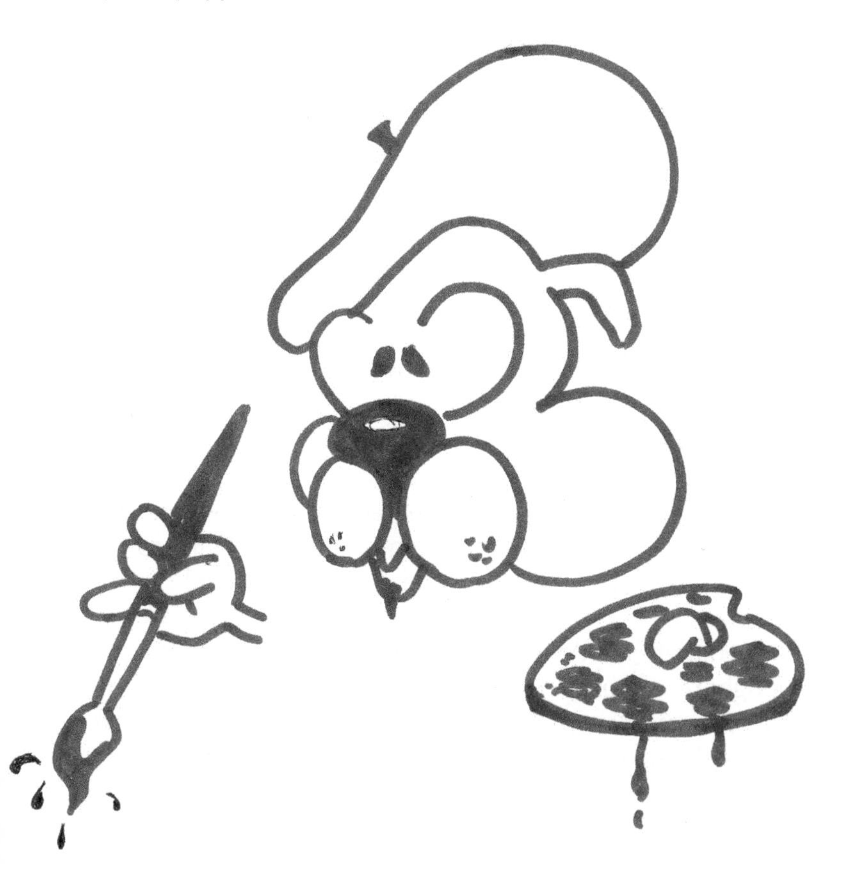

Humming softly to himself, happy to be immersed in art-related tasks

I instinctively combine layers of tastes, I have found, much as The Artist constructs layers, and overlays, in his abstracts. It seems to expand and enhance the dish, the disparate tastes – sweet, sharp, oily, fresh – combining to a harmonious whole.

To the pasta I had also added grated carrot and raisins, for a certain sweetness. Capers for a sudden piquancy. Coriander and lemon zest to lift. Fresh herbs from the garden – thyme on this occasion – and a hint of tamari for a deeper note. We ate, and conversed, and soaked up the sun.

I had prepared no pudding, as The Artist had discovered that some of his favourite clothes had apparently – and unaccountably - shrunk. And, somewhat ruefully, he had decided that his sweet treats should become more occasional.

After lunch, we went straight to The Artist's studio, a happily chaotic place with paints and part-worked canvasses strewn across the floor, boxes of assorted brushes and implements taking up the spaces between, streaks of colour (still drying) on the duvets protecting the carpet. Truly one could say 'An Artist Works Here'.

And how familiar this chaos seemed. Then it dawned on me. It was similar to the chaos now infiltrating my living room. Though much more pronounced. I should beware!

Immediately The Artist's eye went to a pot of paint, newly bought by myself, set apart at the far side of the room. The blackcurrant swatch of paint on the lid had caught his eye. He brightened, instantly.

'Is that jam?' he enquired, hopefully.

Alas, no. It was not.

19 Nature (and an Artist) abhor a vacuum

It was when I had friends invited that I finally put my foot down.

Every surface was claimed by art-related items. The dining table long submerged by framing materials, with the odd canvas lobbed on top. The floor – almost every square inch bar a narrow passage from door to settee, and settee to the garden - was filled with stretched paintings and boxes stacked several deep. Even the chairs were full of The Artist's paperwork. There was simply no room for people.

I insisted that The Artist help me clear everything out of the living room. It was long overdue for a proper clean, as The Artist's very material presence made it impossible to reach nooks and crannies. Or even floor. And I yearned to have my living room back. Clean. Ordered. Spacious. Uncluttered.

The Artist pouted, clearly not happy to be involved in what sounded suspiciously like housework. An increasing number of sighs whilst he toiled signalled his urgent wish to be outside, or painting, or googling clips of his favourite football team. Anything but tidying up!

I gave him the task of moving everything from one end of the room, so I could clean. The Artist took most of it upstairs. He checked with me that his arrangement of paintings in my small bedroom was agreeable. It was indeed a colourful and delightful display. Using every surface again, though. So long as no-one needed to sit on a chair, or move around the room, or do more than peer in at the door, it was fine.

Cleaning finished (and what a relief to see the wood floor gleaming again), The Artist cautiously brought some of the paintings back – by no means all of them - and stacked them surprisingly neatly. Job done!

The Artist immediately made for the door. Surprised, I asked him what had happened to the boxes of framing materials that he had moved.

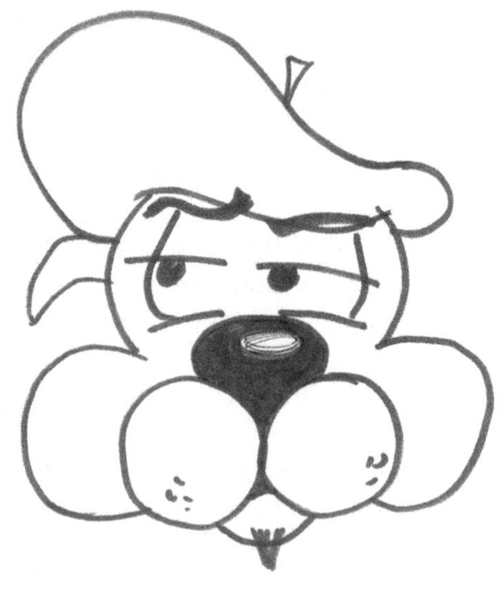

I could detect no trace of remorse at all

'They're in your office,' he said. Straight away, I felt a sense of alarm. My office was already well on the way to being a no go area, as a combination of too little space and insufficient time to organise it (now that a certain Artist was rather commandeering both resources) had meant that chaos was rife. And free floor area considerably limited.

I ran up the stairs to check, before The Artist could make his rapid exit. My wail of dismay could be heard several houses away. I stood at the entrance to the room. I could do no more, as every square inch of floor had been filled.

'You can still get to your printer,' he said, making what he thought was an entirely reasonable point. 'I left room for that'.

Actually, he had not. This was clearly not his forte.

With a sigh, I began to reorganise the boxes.

****

The evening with friends went well, and they were treated to a tour of the (now rather extensive) art gallery. Living room, stairs, landing, bedroom: floors and walls all filled to the brim with vibrant art.

****

A few days later, The Artist prepared the ground for the next step in his unstoppable requisitioning of my home. I had prepared a simple lunch. A potato galette, based on mashed potatoes and swede. To this, I added onion and celery gently sweated in olive oil, plus raisins, grated carrot and fresh coriander. This mixture was then pressed into a frying pan to form a 'cake' and slow-fried until a satisfying crust had built up on the bottom.

Then turned… an operation requiring some dexterity. I placed a plate on top of the pan, inverted it so that the galette dropped elegantly onto the plate, then slid it (the galette, not the plate) back into the frying pan, crusty side up, to complete its transformation.

Served with a salad, in the garden, it was found to be a

satisfying meal. The Artist expressed his appreciation, as always.

He talked about his plans to bring more of his paintings back from their far-flung locations, and whether there might be a place found for them at mine. I agreed, as I knew there were three or four that I particularly loved. And, now that my living room had been cleared, surely there was room for just a few more pieces of art?

I should have known better.

A few days later I arrived home. Unexpectedly, a stack of paintings greeted me in the hall. One of my favourites to the fore.

'Wow!' I exclaimed, unable to contain my delight in the beauty and immediacy of The Artist's work.

My eyes went to the living room, where I could see another of my favourites (a modest seven feet high) awaiting me.

'Wow!' I involuntarily exclaimed again, for the mastery and depth of his work had a very visceral effect on me.

Transported by these two visions of delight, I then caught sight of the rest of my living room. My dining table was piled with dozens of canvasses. The floor had all but disappeared again, under portfolios of assorted work.

Just at that moment, the phone rang. It was The Artist.

'I'm just ringing to say,' he said, in his usual upbeat manner, 'that when you return home this afternoon it is likely to be a rather bitter-sweet experience.'

I could detect no trace of remorse at all.

20 An Artist takes charge…

It was a notable day and I had spent the morning preparing a very special meal for The Artist and I, complete with a very special pudding. And a table laid with my own artistry and care. I had even baked something celebratory for his dog to enjoy.

I was looking forward to some rare time to enjoy a little conversation together, and being able, just for once, to put aside the (surprisingly considerable) amount of work generated for me by this slight figure.

Everything was prepared. But – this was The Artist, after all and it was not to go to plan. Just ten minutes before he was due to make an appearance, the phone rang.

'I'm sorry to say I can't get there,' he said. 'I had just set off from the studio, when my car stopped moving. I have to wait here for the breakdown people.'

I took in the situation. There was no way that all my preparation was going to waste. In moments, I hatched an alternative plan.

'Well, in that case, I'll bring the meal to you. And we can eat while you wait for them.'

Plan agreed, I set about turning the repast into Artist Meals on Wheels. Packing up all the china currently waiting on the table so as not to entirely lose the ambiance I had conjured, I transferred the meal in my car to his studio.

Squatting on the floor, amidst paint, brushes and part-completed canvasses, we enjoyed our repast.

The main part of the meal was Inam Bayeldi, a sumptuous Middle-Eastern dish of aubergine with herbs and tomatoes. Gratifyingly simple to prepare, the baking transforms it into silky, smoky mouthfuls of utter delight.

This was both echoed and counterpointed by the slow roasted tomatoes, peppers and squash. The sprigs of fresh rosemary punched out a zesty tone, whilst the olive oil softened and fragranced it all. A big pot of simple boiled potatoes (an abiding favourite of This Artist) completed the main course.

It was polished off, whilst enjoying the contrast of the discerning presentation of the meal with the rather bohemian setting.

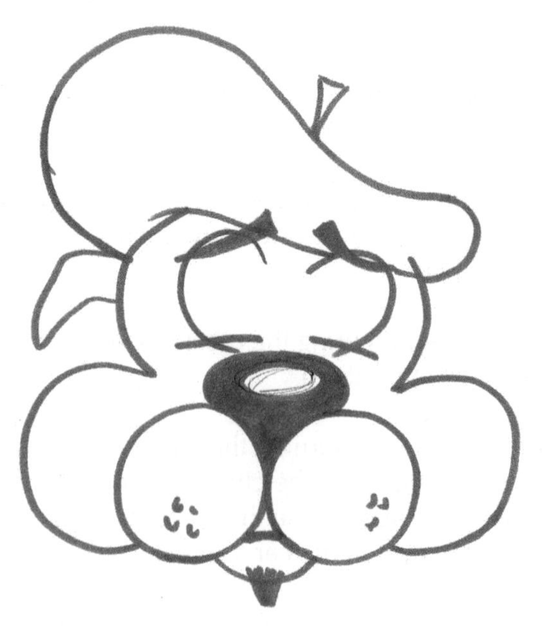

There was a long, long silence, punctuated just occasionally with an appreciative 'mmm' as The Artist savoured every mouthful

'That was very nice indeed,' The Artist exclaimed. After he had checked – several times – that there was no possibility of more potatoes to be had, he added, 'Did you say something about pudding?'

I had. Chocolate and Lemon pots, a dessert of my own devising. I knew The Artist would truly appreciate this one. I had used dark chocolate soya dessert as a base – so tasty, it would be hard to recognise it as vegan for those who didn't know about such distinctions, or the reasons why it might be important for some.

Some creaminess was added courtesy of soya yoghurt and a good splodge of oat cream. The lemon zing was a simple matter of lemon zest and juice. Served in a ramekin, and finished with a few fresh blueberries on top plus grated vegan chocolate, it was truly a pudding worthy of any top notch restaurant.

There was a long, long silence, punctuated just occasionally with an appreciative 'mmm' as The Artist savoured every mouthful. And scraped the ramekin with his spoon with studied care. The sweetness of the taste contrasted vividly with the bitterness of the imminent diagnosis of his car.

****

The car was a write off!

There was no question but that I would have to become The Artist's chauffeur. Until he could find some means of transport to his liking. For me, this meant getting up early to ferry Artist (plus dog) to his studio...

As was his way, The Artist took it as his due. But never failed to show his appreciation in rather unconventional ways:

A cinema voucher I might be able to use.

Some scarves he thought I would like.

And one day, some tins of fairtrade beans he had bought as a thank you to me. I did take that last gift to be an expression of very high esteem indeed.

It took much longer than either of us expected to get The Artist mobile again – a saga that deserves its own tale, at some point. But after a month, with still no solution in sight, I decided it would make more sense to allow my car to be driven by The Artist too.

Not more than a day or so afterwards The Artist began to insist on driving. He mumbled something about giving me a chance to relax while he took the strain.

Days turned to weeks, and yet another month went by, with still no decision on a replacement car. His insistence on driving continued.

One day I had the temerity to sit in the driver's seat. The Artist gently stood his ground until the car was ceded.

I decided I needed to understand this intransigence. It was my car, after all. So, as we – he, I and his dog – walked to the car one morning, I took the plunge.

'So what's this insistence on being the driver about?' I began. 'Is it a man thing, about needing to be in charge? Or is it really as you say, about wanting to do something nice for me?'

The Artist smiled, sweetly. 'It's about doing something nice for you,' he said, with all apparent sincerity.

He then nodded over his shoulder towards his elderly dog. 'And for her.'

He said nothing more, until I quizzed him further. 'Well,' he said. 'You drive much faster than I do. She doesn't feel comfortable with it.'

And thus, the penny dropped. I suspected the benefit was not mine at all and his consideration was indeed entirely for his dog.

If so, I could detect no remorse in him at all.

As always.

21 Playful Moments

The Artist particularly prized those moments in which he could be playful, or enjoy an uplifting interlude. They lifted his spirits considerably.

He had recently facilitated a 'walk with an artist's eye' for a group. I had been allowed to borrow his prized camera for it, and – with his guidance on how to look at the scene - had been rather pleased with my results.

We later examined the photos I had taken. 'Oooh, look,' I exclaimed at the first image that came up. 'That's a very good photo. I'm really pleased with that one.'

The Artist solemnly agreed. 'Yes,' he said, 'That one is good.'

I looked at the next photo. And looked again, in puzzlement. For I could not recognise it at all.

'Oh, what's this one?' I wondered aloud. 'It's another very good photo. I really like what I've captured. But I just don't recall taking it.'

'Actually, that one's mine,' The Artist said. 'As was the first one, I'm afraid...'

****

Playful moments were not the sole preserve of The Artist, though he was - demonstrably - rather practised in them.

I had the opportunity, one day, to turn The Artist's culinary quirks onto himself. Whilst making his favourite hot soya milk for him to drink, I spied a dried fig, the last in a packet.

As he was so fond of including an incongruous ingredient in his cooking (his current fad being for dried fruit of some description), plus his snacking habit lately had been to demolish whole packets of that fruit, I simply couldn't resist. In went the fig.

I presented the beverage to The Artist, with no comment. But a gleeful smile spread itself, inside. I waited for the moment of discovery.

The Artist drank slowly, absorbed with thoughts of a painting he was thinking of creating. Eventually he encountered the fig at the bottom of his mug.

'Oooh, that's nice,' he cooed, completely unphased. 'Whatever it is.'

****

For the most part, one of us would have sole charge of the kitchen when preparing a lunch. I would often be shooed away by The Artist, so that he would be free to invoke his culinary muse without hindrance.

In my view, this consisted of little more than arranging the more ageing contents of fridge and cupboard on the work surface (as this fitted well with his ethos of not wishing to waste even the smallest scrap), along with a 'wild card' that had caught his eye whilst rummaging. And, with these random ingredients selected, to invent some wildly improbable means of combining them.

Once, when time and inspiration were short, I suggested we

might just have a bowl of baked beans. I rather fancied the simple, sweet, tomato taste that I was already sampling in my mind.

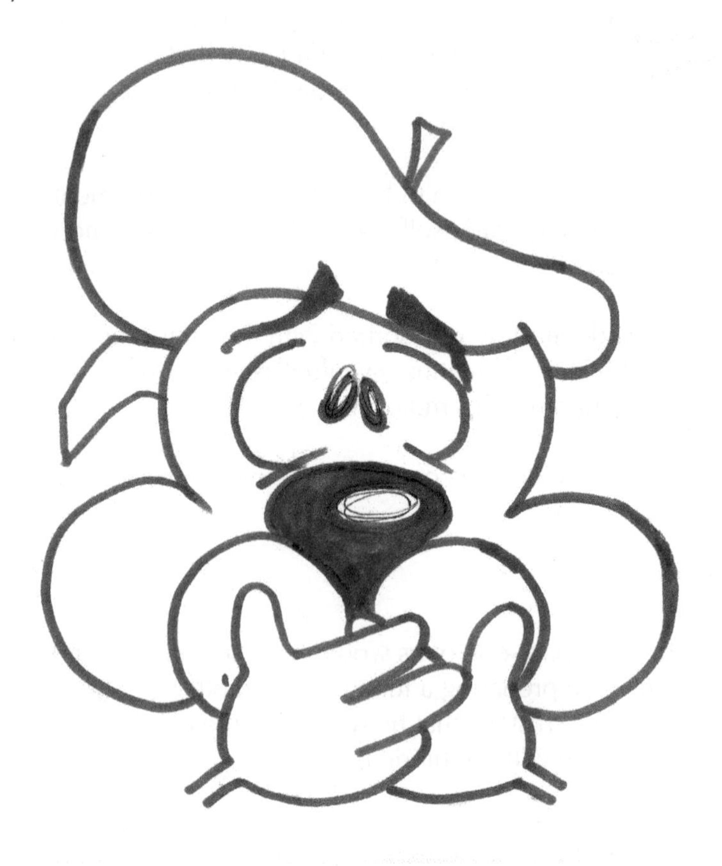

With these random cooking ingredients selected, he would invent some wildly improbable means of combining them

The Artist volunteered to prepare it, and the imagined bowl soon appeared. But the very first mouthful dashed my expectations.

'Euughhh!' I exclaimed. 'What have you done? There's vinegar in this!' My sustenance had been, to my mind, spoilt.

The Artist duly accepted my comment, which he clearly took to be an accolade.

'Well yes,' he said, with some gravity. 'I don't like plain. It's just not interesting. So I added some chutney.'

I tried another mouthful, and gradually, reluctantly, adjusted myself to the novel taste. Perhaps it was not all that bad, after all. Maybe...

Then my fork prodded something solid. My heart sank. Was there another culinary surprise to be endured?

'And what's this?' I asked, not quite sure that I really wanted to know.

'Oh, that's just a rice cake,' he explained, nonchalantly. As if rice cakes were often to be found under a pile of baked beans.

On this occasion, I had reached the limit of my tolerance. I dubiously prodded the soggy, disintegrating disc and rapidly came to a decision. I hoisted it out of the bowl. The Artist clearly liked that sort of thing. So he could jolly well eat it.

Which he did. With all apparent relish.

****

Occasionally we attempted to cook something together. Since The Artist was involved, the experience generally included an unpredictable variation on (my) vision. Or, more usually, an entirely predictable fading of his attention and subsequent disappearance in search of something far more amusing.

I thought we might make something with lentils – always a tasty base for a meal, and gratifyingly simple to cook.

Beluga lentils are considered to be the 'caviar' of the lentil family (hence the name) as the small black discs glisten once cooked and could almost be mistaken for the appearance of caviar. They have a more refined taste than regular lentils, too.

I cooked some in water, with a bay leaf for extra aroma. Whilst they were softening, I sautéed onion and celery in olive oil for a silky, fragrant mix. At the same time, I quick roasted slices of butternut squash in the oven, again with a little olive oil brushed over to encourage a softness of texture.

When each of the separate ingredients were ready, I combined them, together with some grated carrot for freshness, and tamari to link the flavours together. Delicious!

Whilst I did this, I left The Artist to organise pudding. Eating it was his favourite point in the day. So it seemed entirely fitting.

However, I was so absorbed in my own culinary creating, that I entirely failed to oversee the direction his was taking.

He was only too happy to explain, whilst I dubiously poked the mush he had brought out (and with a triumphant flourish, too).

He had fried slices of banana in sunflower oil. 'Enough to make them nice and mushy,' he emphasised. To this, he added sliced dried figs (his current dried fruit passion) along with the remains of the crystallised ginger he loved to have as an occasional, or at that time, fairly frequent, treat. A few minutes cooking to amalgamate the flavours, and the dish was done.

'Then I just served it with soya yoghurt under it, and on top,' he said, in his gentle, matter of fact, 'doesn't everyone do this?' tone of voice.

I have to say, it was not as bad as it sounded. It was actually rather tasty.

But I promptly dubbed the dish 'The Artist's Bananas'.

Because there are times when that really does seem to me to be an entirely fitting description!

22 The Artist Refusing to be Labelled

It does indeed seem to me that managing An Artist calls for a considerable amount of tolerance to be employed.

In addition to any straightforward discussions on the practicalities of a project, there always seems to be some indelible foible (or dare I say, stubborn refusal?) that needs to be sensitively, or sometimes not so sensitively, navigated.

We had another major exhibition to prepare for. A respected restaurant - the whole two floors – were to be filled with The Artist's abstract paintings.

We began the lengthy process of creating the display. The Artist immersed himself happily in the task of selecting from his archive of work which ones would be included in this collection.

Absorbed in a reflective reverie, he spent quite some time padding around my house (for many of them now resided in my home) leafing through stacks of paintings, considering their respective impact and building a mental image of how they might combine to create a particular ambiance in the restaurant itself.

The curating was completed, with a few extra included to give a degree of choice for the hanging. In some alchemical way, it isn't until artwork and venue are actually introduced to each other that the final selection of work becomes clear.

The next stage was to prepare them for display. Each painting - and there were thirty to be tackled - had to be scrutinised to be sure that it was in pristine condition, before carefully washing it to brighten and tighten the canvas.

The Artist was quite happy to be absorbed in this act of homage to his art; lovingly bathing each one, contemplating old favourites anew, placing each in a sunny spot to dry (for with the combined requirements of water and sun, a garden was surely the perfect place to be doing this).

Hours passed. My garden shimmered with colour and form. The Artist hummed contentedly to himself as he worked. He quite seemed to have forgotten about his usual, frequent, needs for 'a little something', that ordinarily would seem so necessary to punctuate his day. Clearly his senses were being fed in an altogether more nurturing way.

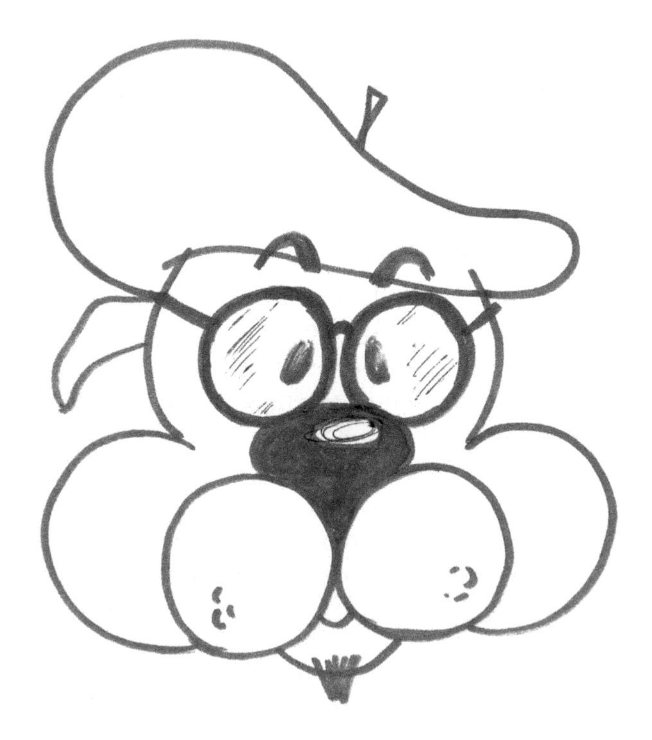

The Artist was quite happy to be absorbed in this act of homage to his art

But that didn't mean that I could forgo the actual feeding of This Artist. Unconsciously mirroring his activities, I gathered together those ingredients that called to me, from the selection available, in some unspoken act of curation.

My dish, I decided, was to be formed with cauliflower as its inspiration. I sautéed some seeds in the pan for an aromatic underpinning: mustard, onion and fenugreek seeds together with curry leaves to give an Asian slant. Sliced onion, celery and grated carrot soon joined them, the glistening seeds delicately flecking the vegetables.

The cauliflower, separated into florets, brought a pleasing array of colour, as if this were an expressionist painting: pools of white, pale green, orange intermingled in interesting, yet changing, patterns.

A contingent of vibrant green came next: spinach, plenty of fresh coriander, green pepper and pak choi plus some finely chopped chilli to counterpoint the cool freshness of the vegetables.

The finishing touch, and in some ways the most important as it is the means of bringing the separate ingredients into a coherent composition, was the sauce. Which I discovered, through slowly tasting, and contemplating, merely needed to be the zest and juice of a lime for sharpness, and vegan yoghurt for creaminess.

The Artist was ready for the repast. We sat in the garden, amidst all his paintings, content with the outcome of our day, each appreciating what the other had created.

****

The day of hanging arrived. The Artist carefully loaded his paintings into my car, and that of his exhibition assistant. I drove straight to the restaurant, whilst he and assistant called in quickly to pick something up from his studio.

I waited. And waited. I was surrounded by paintings, but lacking a certain Artist. Puzzled, I called, to be reassured that they were almost arrived. It was only later that the assistant confessed that The Artist's navigating skills had led them – sadly – quite astray, and the very short journey between studio and restaurant had turned into an unexpectedly lengthy tour of the city.

The team now gathered, we focused on installing the art before diners were to appear. The Artist and assistant formed the creative team, involved with decisions about how to arrange the display, and putting them up. I, consistent with the manager's role, provided some much needed quality control whilst I also created the catalogue of art on display.

Some of the paintings needed to be restrung, to allow them to sit at the right height in the room. This task fell to me. The assistant, at the top of the ladder, installed the hooks, and hung the paintings. The Artist stood back to survey the whole scene, and, mostly, simply pointed to where he wanted things to go.

We paused to admire the change in the feel of the restaurant, with so much art on display. As we surveyed the scene, the calm majesty of the Georgian building, graced with 26 of his abstract paintings, showed them in all their splendour. Displayed in their rightful setting, with each one's true qualities now able to be fully seen.

Artistic pause completed, I reminded the duo that each

painting still needed to be labelled: one to show viewers the details of title and price, plus the contentious Artist's label on the back to confirm its provenance.

The Artist pouted, as he so often did, when confronted with this particularly tedious task. He resisted, still not fully convinced of their merit. I insisted, certain of their necessity.

The Artist ceded, with a sigh. He and his assistant duly began to attach said labels. Having gained victory on this matter, I discretely gave them space.

A while later, my own tasks brought me close to where they were working. By chance, I picked up the pile of labels they were using. And immediately realised that something was amiss.

'But this one's not signed!' I exclaimed. I held the label in question aloft. 'Were the others? Look, I have all the signed ones still here.'

The Artist exchanged a look of complicity with the assistant. 'Oh, I'm sure they are,' he claimed, clearly not wanting to do this tedious task all over again.

I judiciously let it go, knowing I could substitute signed labels at a later date, but removed the remaining unsigned ones from the pile. Just to be sure.

Labelling completed, The Artist presented himself as having finished. We toured the display together, admiring, commenting, appreciating, and doing a final straightening.

'Hmmm,' I said. 'Did you realise that every single one of the pricing labels is askew.'

'I know,' The Artist said, his chest puffed with some degree of pride. 'I like it like that. All part of the creative process.'

I smiled to myself. I did not share his view, but I knew that this was something we would always be at odds about.

I gently cajoled him. 'Can we perhaps agree for the future that the creative part stays within the painting? And that the display part carries some precision?'

The Artist pulled a face.

He did so need his acts of rebellion.

23 The Artist creates chaos. Again!

No matter how substantial the degree of chaos just created by The Artist, the upbeat (and rather hopeful, even pleased) way in which he confessed to it always made it seem impossible to do anything but smile indulgently at him.

We had pulled out many of his paintings from their storage places to show a dealer who wanted to see a wider range of The Artist's work.

My entire house, and the shady parts of the garden, had been commandeered by canvasses, which The Artist lovingly unrolled, one by one, to reveal images we had both long forgotten, but were greeted anew with exclamations of delight.

Artist, manager and dealer spent a happy afternoon together in delightful discovery. There's simply nothing better than looking at art in quantity for lifting one's spirits to a higher plane. Well, with This Artist's art, anyway, for each painting contains some essential part of his soul.

Dealer gone, I asked The Artist to put everything back, whilst I got on with preparing something simple for us to eat. Shepherd's Pie, that quintessentially comforting British dish, was quite easy to recast in a vegan version. And had the advantage of plentiful potatoes – always a winner as far as The Artist was concerned.

A substantial quantity of potatoes were thus duly boiled and mashed with olive oil and soya milk. The underlying part of the dish was soon created by sautéing onions, celery and carrots (all cut into small chunks) with garlic and fresh thyme.

To this, I added freshly cooked green lentils, and a handful of roughly chopped walnuts for depth of taste and texture. Finally, a good slug of tamari and quite a lot of the lentil cooking water, as it is important for the mixture to remain moist enough to yield a tasty gravy when served.

Baking it was delightfully simple. The lentil mix occupied the lower layer in a large baking dish, whilst the mash provided a fluffy layer on top. Around 45 minutes in a moderate oven and a repast to satisfy even the most demanding of Artists would be ready.

Diligently, whilst I cooked, The Artist transported armfuls of paintings up the stairs and back into my office. It took quite a few trips to do so. But eventually the ground floor of my house emerged into view once more.

I should have known from too many other experiences that The Artist's forte was not organisation (i.e. putting things away).

Certainly, not in putting things away tidily. And most definitely not in making sensible use of storage space. My blissful ignorance was soon to be punctured.

'You'll never guess what!' The Artist chirped, as he came down the stairs.

'When I put all the canvasses back, the shelf in your cupboard sort of collapsed.'

He beamed widely as he shared this news. Whether it was with some pride in his achievement, or in the hope of diverting any potential furore, was rather hard to discern.

'But it's all right,' he continued. 'Because if we just take out the box on the shelf underneath, we can let it all collapse onto the lower shelf and everything will be fine.'

I paused to consider this novel suggestion. And just as quickly discarded it. Examining the aftermath, I could see that The Artist had simply put every single canvas back onto one lone shelf, instead of the several places they had originally been entrusted to. No shelf could possibly have born that quantity of art.

It was clear that I needed to upgrade the robustness of my office. With The Artist steadily infiltrating it, it was time for a major reorganisation, so that I could actually continue to work in it whilst providing better storage for all this art.

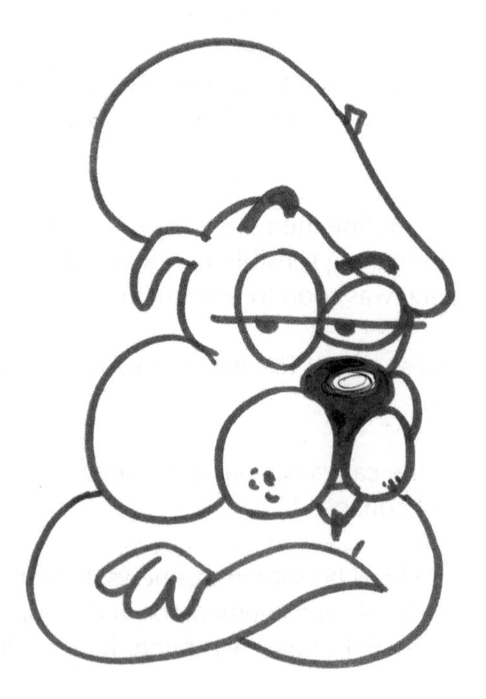

Whether it was with some pride in his achievement, or in the hope of diverting any potential furore, was rather hard to discern

And so, broken cupboard having been condemned, I ordered two new ones to replace it.

****

A few days later, we set about emptying the office. No small feat. And clearly too reminiscent of housework, as The Artist had optimistically attempted to wriggle out of it, fervently suggesting that some urgent need for him to be away on that particular day would undoubtedly occur. I put my foot down.

Before long, the contents of my office were clogging up every room on the upper floor. Bathroom and bedrooms were completely out of action now that every inch of floor was overflowing.

Predictably, within minutes of my new units arriving, The Artist claimed them for himself. I turned to see him quietly putting his canvasses into them.

'Just hold on there!' I exclaimed, privately quite amused but not about to let on. 'These are my units! That one is now yours.' I gestured to an old shelving unit that was perfect for his canvasses.

I was just showing you how it would look,' he pretended. But, temporarily thwarted in his ambitions, he obediently filled the designated shelves instead.

It was only some hours later, having been pondering how best to arrange everything back into the newly arranged office, that I realised that – naturally – The Artist was going to have to have one of the new units after all, as that was the only one with the right configuration for all his bits.

I sighed, and sadly resigned myself to my fate.

24 The Artist chooses a car. Or does he...

The Artist's car had died. A means of transport was definitely needed, so we began the search for a suitable replacement.

But it soon became clear that The Artist was not about to make a quick decision. Or, indeed, a decision of any kind.

He seemed to require a vehicle that simply didn't exist. Something large enough to transport his paintings (which could be quite sizeable, to say the least). But small enough, and frugal enough, to be viable as a daily runaround. Cheap to buy, to accord with his philosophy of modest needs. Plus space for his much-loved dog to feel comfortable.

Our search took in most of the car dealers in the locality. Did he want a car version of a van, with its practical load area? Or a small van, basic but reliable? An estate, even, plus trailer for when larger items needed to be lugged?

Much like Goldilocks trying the three bears' porridge, The Artist simply could not choose. There was something not to his liking with each that we tried.

Weeks went by. I did what I could to assist with the search, researching The Artist's latest inclination and finding examples for sale. But it happened all too frequently that, by the time I offered my findings, his thinking had long since moved in a different, and generally unexpected, direction.

Clearly this was to be a slow, and organic, process. And evidently The Artist was experiencing no urgency of any kind in this matter. Perhaps the fact that he now had the use of my car had some small bearing on this.

I sighed, and resolved to be patient.

It was time for lunch. Always a welcome part of the day, and a chance to try new ideas with food. I fancied something potato-based, as both The Artist and I shared a love for this vegetable. I invited him to cook with me, though without expectation of any sustained effort on his part, as I had learned from experience that his attention on anything that was not Art (or football, or googled music clips) could be rather temporary.

I dry-toasted mustard and sesame seeds, to bring out the oils that contained their taste. Then sliced an onion, grated a couple of baking potatoes and a carrot. These were all mixed gently together with salt plus a few oats to help bind the mix together - just slightly - when it cooked. I wanted it to stay light and airy, not mashed together into a lump.

The flavourings were delegated to The Artist, as this surely required some artistic deliberations. I suggested fresh mint and chilli and, perhaps foolishly, left him to this task.
Task completed, The Artist had disappeared. I could hear strains of music from the living room. Clearly he had found my laptop again.

I chuckled and heated olive oil in the frying pan, lightly adding the mix, complete with Artist-supplied flavours, and gently firmed it with a fork. It needed to be cooked on a moderate heat, so the potato was soft by the time the bottom crust had browned, and the mixture held itself together.

When the time came to turn the potato cake, the simplest method, I have found, is to put a plate on top of the pan and invert it, so that the contents plop onto the plate. It is then reasonably easy to slide it back into the pan, intact and crust uppermost, to cook on the other side.

I served it with marinated peppers, a delicatessen item that is easy to make oneself but if time is short, almost as good to buy ready-made in a jar. The oily richness of the peppers contrasted well with the simpler taste of the potatoes. Some dressed salad leaves completed the meal.

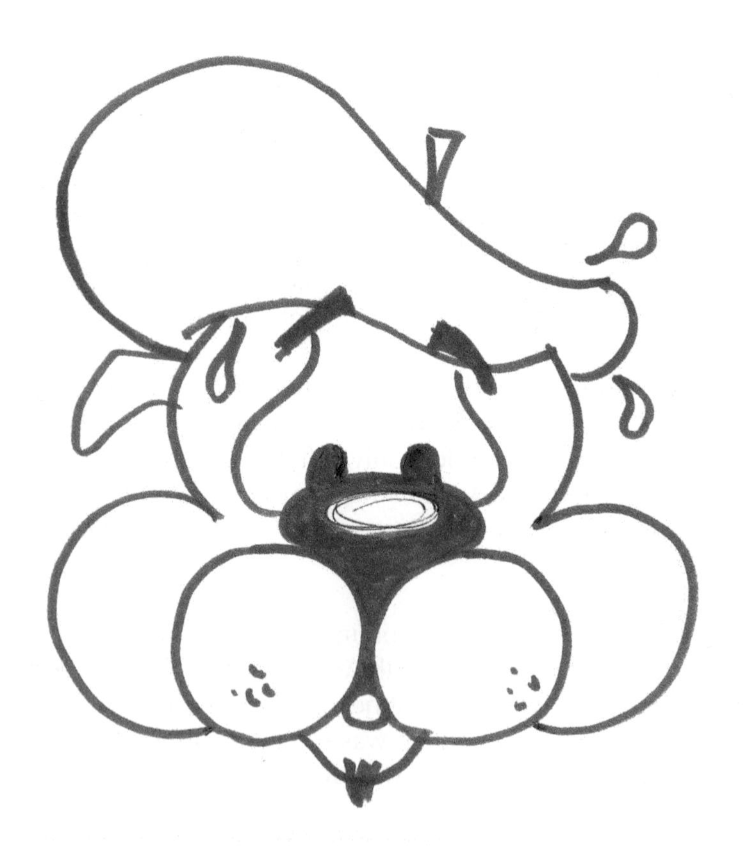

Who had put far too much chilli in the potato cake?
My money was on a certain Artist

We sat down to eat. I took a forkful. My eyes immediately watered. The main topic of conversation over lunch had just become clear. It was to ascertain which of us it might have been who had put far too much chilli in the potato cake.

My money was on a certain Artist.

Said Artist simply shrugged, contriving to maintain his habitual air of innocence. And deftly changed the subject to one that was more to his liking.

'I've just been thinking,' he interjected, 'that perhaps what I need is a campervan...'

25 Baked beans and beloved companions

The Artist's beloved canine companion of 17 years was ailing.

Such was his devotion to her, he vowed he would not leave her unattended for a moment, as he could not forgive himself if she were to fall, and be in distress.

Self-imposed exile in place, there was nothing for it but for me to create a temporary office in The Artist's kitchen for the duration.

Now this was NOT a kitchen as I, or anyone, would recognise. Where were the condiments? Where were the utensils? Indeed where was the food! Austerity and minimalism were indeed the prevailing theme. I searched the cupboards in forlorn hope.

I installed my laptop next to his on the kitchen table and endeavoured to concentrate on the promotion of matters artistic. And each day, I smuggled in some vital item of kitchen equipment. A saucepan. Some plates. A grater (on the use of which The Artist required some instruction). And, above all, food!

As with all of us when we are unwell, the invalid's appetite was changing. Vegetarian for all of her 17 years, and demonstrably bursting with health till recently as a result, like her human she was really quite particular. I would be despatched frequently to buy new tidbits to tempt her to eat.

Of major interest were the vegetarian sausages that came with a certain make of beans. However, the beans themselves were markedly less exciting. This meant that every time I considered cooking at The Artist's, there were always several cans of beans piling up in the fridge, sans sausages, and in urgent need of use.

I sighed, knowing that The Artist abhorred waste. And set myself to finding ever-more inventive ways of hiding baked beans (in quantity) within my cooking.

I attempted a stir-fry. The usual vegetables as a base: onion, celery, carrot. Some sweet potato to add a soft, yielding texture. Plenty of fresh coriander for zing. I added sliced green cabbage, and French beans for variety. And a little water to loosen the mix.

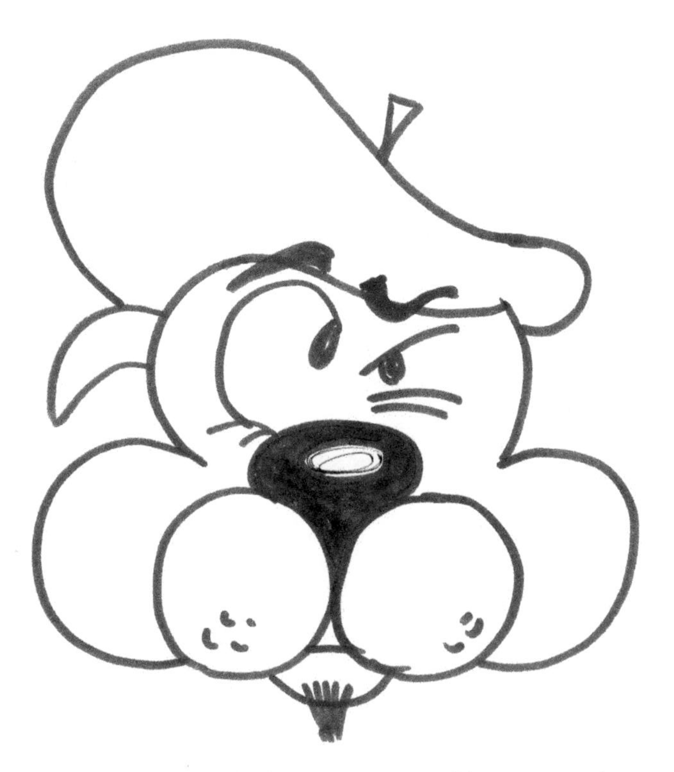

Absentmindedly, for he had a concept in mind for a new sculpture, he took a forkful. And ate it all with quite some relish

And then, the moment of truth. Before I could lose my nerve, I closed my eyes and emptied in a can. In truth, the tomato and seasoning of the sauce provided quite an agreeable background to the freshness of the vegetables. And beans – in this case haricot, of course - were not such an unusual partnering. A fried potato cake completed the repast.

Relieved, I called The Artist to the table. Absentmindedly, for he had a concept in mind for a new sculpture, he took a forkful.

'This is great,' he said. And ate it all with quite some relish.

It was no surprise at all that he found the taste agreeable. After all, his own cooking style often included 'hidden' beans.

I started to eat, too. And, to my own surprise, it really wasn't too bad at all.

26 When personal desires collide

The Artist had lost interest in his favourite chocolate soya dessert, since his culinary passions tended to be intense but of a temporary nature. So I had not bought any for a while.

But on a recent shopping trip they caught my eye again and I decided I'd buy a selection of the flavours on offer. I would enjoy them even if An Artist deigned not to.

It was only a day later that he sat down next to me, having been in the kitchen. Unsupervised. In his hand, already half consumed, was a soya dessert. He tried, not too convincingly, to pretend innocence.

Clearly he considered it to have been pre-destined. 'It fell into my hand when I opened the cupboard,' he exclaimed. 'And who am I to resist the fates...'

Who, indeed. For this rather charming openness to the vagaries of the moment spoke of The Artist's deeply-held approach to life and his art. Rather than seeking to impose his stamp on the day, The Artist's philosophical stance encouraged a willingness to savour and be influenced by whatever might come his way.

By stepping back in this way from his pre-conceptions and personal desires, The Artist sought to remain unbiased enough to allow a profound quality to emerge, free to find its own form, whilst he painted. And this, to my view, contributed to the depth to be found in his art.

In daily life The Artist remained delightfully fallible in this aim, though, as there were particular enthusiasms that irresistibly called him away from his chosen discipline of floating freely. Puddings being one such. But, even then, his expressions of delight retained an openness and innocence that were simply enchanting. And quite impossible to not feel indulgent towards.

Football was another of The Artist's passions. After an al fresco lunch one day with friends, he expressed his appreciation for the meal, as always. Then quietly slid away. Before long, we could hear the sounds of football from the house. Clearly, he had commandeered my laptop again, and was googling match highlights.

A while later, he came back, flushed with excitement, a huge grin on his face.

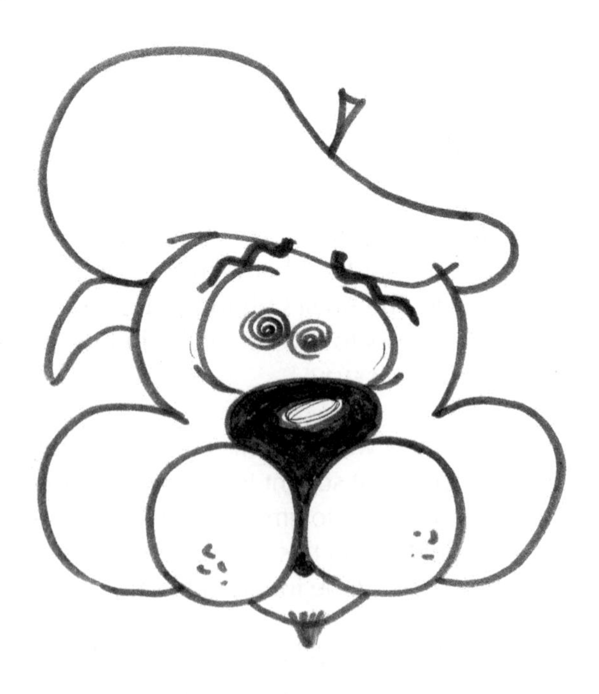

"I've just watched every single goal scored by my team this year. Eighty six of them! It was wonderful!"

'You look really happy,' I said.

'Yes,' The Artist agreed enthusiastically. 'I've just watched every single goal scored by my team this year. Eighty six of them! It was wonderful!'

The Artist was rather partial to treats of this nature, for they lifted his spirits considerably. And smoothed his path into the next bit of work to tackle, as his free-floating way meant he became engaged in something through being inspired, rather than by grimly knuckling down. A circumstance, as it happens, that was generally met with a fair amount of grumbling, should his manager ever insist.

The inevitable collision between The Artist's contentment to relinquish his desires for any particular outcome and his personal predilection for treats (and if they were unfamiliar, so much the better) took place one summer's day.

It was late in the morning. We'd spoken on the phone, having had our respective business matters to attend to. But soon it would be time to meet again for our joint care of matters artistic.

'Will you be wanting lunch?' I enquired.

'No, I'm fine,' The Artist replied. 'I've been snacking all morning. I don't need anything more.'

Foolishly, I took The Artist at his word. As it happened, coincidentally, that morning I had come across something quite novel to cook. So I felt I had the time to experiment, since I didn't need to produce a coherent lunch.

Avocado fries. What an amazing concept! I had bought an

avocado that had turned out to be still unripe, but needed to be used now it had been cut open. And as a result had found this fascinating recipe. But it called for egg and wheat flour, neither of which were possible for my perennial lunch guest.

How to make them both tasty and vegan? I had a bash. A crisp crust would be a very good start. I cut the avocado into chip-size slices. Instead of using eggs to bind it all, I coated them with ground flax mixed into a thick batter with water. Then dipped the avocado into the polenta.

Sprinkled with olive oil and simply baked, they looked quite interesting. And, purely in the interests of research, of course, I have to confess that I ate the lot.

****

When the Artist arrived later that afternoon, I told him of my new dish, and what a shame it was that he had not needed to eat. He could see that he had clearly missed out.

'But you didn't tell me you were going to do something new and interesting!' he spluttered. 'I'd have come for lunch if I'd known.'

The Artist had known I had been tied up with a project all morning. The light was beginning to dawn. He had probably assumed I had not had time to cook.

'Are you meaning you declined because thought you might have been getting plain beans, or something equally uninteresting?' I chuckled.

The Artist didn't need to say a word. The look on his face rather confirmed the matter.

27 An Artist's Delight

Much like a shark is said to need to be in constant motion in order to remain alive, so change, to This Artist, was mostly something to be embraced. Each new circumstance presented a fresh perspective on life. And generally would spark an idea or two for yet another painting.

And change was indeed in the air. It was time for The Artist to relinquish his current studio. It had served him well, providing a nurturing cocoon for his Artist's endeavours in a time of transition and uncertainty.

But he had outgrown it. Or rather, it might be more accurate to say, the scale of his painting ambitions (for he liked the freedom and movement offered by a large canvas) had rather outstripped the available floor space.

As the time grew closer, we gradually transferred his finished work to my house. It really didn't seem possible to squeeze any more art into my home. But somehow, when The Artist arrived, cooing 'Just a few more...', space was found.

****

A similar delight in new discoveries extended to the matter of puddings for this decidedly sweet-toothed Artist. It became a daily challenge for me to find a new (and blissful) combination of the vegan and wheat-free staples that were now regular inhabitants of my kitchen.

On this occasion, I decided on fruit as the base. I have long enjoyed the freshness (yet with a comforting, sweet warmth) that comes from lightly cooking fruit in water and little else.

I chopped an apple and (after zesting it) sliced an orange, and added fruit plus zest to a small amount of water. The apple provided a neutral base, the orange brought a high note. After some thought, I added dried prunes to bring an deeper earthy tone to the mix, as well as the requisite sweetness.

When cooked, and allowed a few minutes to cool slightly, I stirred in some of The Artist's chocolate soya dessert and roughly the same amount of vanilla soya custard. It would have been equally good to have just added some soya yoghurt.

The Artist suddenly came to life. It seemed he really liked this pudding. He even said as much. He ate, with all his attention on it. Then scraped the sides of his bowl, over and over, until it was all gone. He remained intent on his bowl - tentatively, wondering how I might react – when I saw him extend his tongue, and delicately (like a cat) licked the sides.

Although deceptively simple to make, the resulting pudding was clearly something of a triumph. I promptly called it 'Artist's Delight'.

The obligatory second helping was obtained, for I knew by now to always cook more than I might think is needed. This, too, disappeared all too rapidly. And then, his bowl was offered out, Oliver-like, for a third.

He was soon protesting about 'cruelty to Artists' on finding out that I had not thought to cook an even greater quantity. And that he had eaten it all.

****

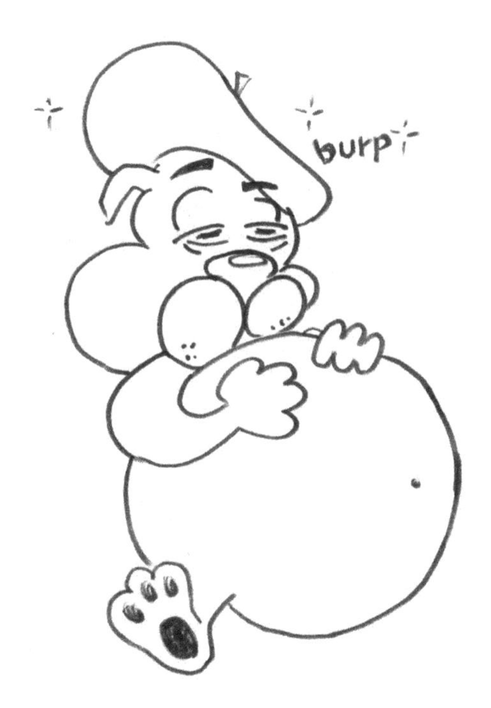

He was soon protesting about 'cruelty to Artists' on finding out that I had not thought to cook an even greater quantity. And that he had eaten it all

The day arrived when we needed to finally vacate The Artist's studio, and return it from its happily artistic jumble to a clean and empty space. I brought a variety of cleaning implements, aware that it had been quite some time since floor had been glimpsed.

Together, we emptied the room. But all the packing and cleaning clearly seemed rather too much like housework to The Artist. I could see he was not in his comfort zone, for, periodically, he would discover some forgotten delight that immediately captured his easily seduced attention.

'Ooh look!' he exclaimed. 'There's some crystallised ginger at the back of this shelf.' Ginger was one of The Artist's abiding treats. An entire packet could mysteriously vanish within moments, if not carefully rationed.

'I didn't know I had this,' he continued, suddenly very happy indeed. 'No point in packing it. I'd better just eat it now'

In such things, The Artist's world did not change. 'So, is that your contribution to clearing out your studio? Eating the ginger?' I smiled, aware that his capacity for emptying and tidying had possibly already been reached.

'Probably!' he beamed, exuding such a degree of charm that it was simply impossible to be cross with him.

'I'll do the hard bit, he continued, evidently under the impression that he was pulling his weight, 'and take the boxes to the car whilst you hoover. You know how unpractical I am...'

I did. It was indeed true. So I hoovered.

It took some considerable while.

But eventually it was done, and I put the last few things in the corridor, waiting for The Artist to carry them down. The hoover took its place next to them. When next I looked, everything had gone.

Except for one - noticeable - item.

The Artist came back to find me, clearly puzzled.

'So, did you leave the hoover in the room then?' he asked.

The fact that The Artist remembered that a hoover had even been present represented, in my view, a sign of progress.

'No,' I replied, evenly. 'It's that big blue thing sitting right there.' I pointed to just a few feet away. 'You took everything else to the car. Was the hoover somehow invisible to you?'

Clearly, this had been the case. The Artist looked, dutifully, to where I was pointing. Suddenly, as if for the first time, he seemed to recognise it.

I hid my smile.

28 A Summer's Treat

It was a rare sunny day. I had declared an impromptu summer celebration after being seduced by the sumptuous English strawberries I had discovered in the supermarket.

I'd also been curious for some time to try agave syrup as a new form of natural sweetening, and had treated myself to a bottle of this cactus-derived elixir.

Coincidentally, it had been on my mind in the past few days that I hadn't made any spelt bread for The Artist for a while. The thought had particularly occurred to me when I had recently caught him staring rather gloomily at his regular substitute of oat crackers.

In addition, that very morning I had had an epiphany! Oat cream on top of bread and jam was pretty well near as damn it cream tea quality. And as the Artist would have put it, without the suffering.

All of these strands combined serendipitously into a sudden desire to make scones. Vegan spelt scones, of course, with fresh strawberries and oat cream as a topping. I fancied I could already taste them.

I searched for a recipe which might give me a springboard for my own improvisation and to suit what I had available.

And so, I set to work. I mixed spelt flour, salt, baking powder and crushed cardamon seeds. Coconut oil helped it form a crumble-like dough. To this I added mixed spice plus ingredients which would give the scones a complexity of taste, such as poppy seeds, dried prunes, figs and walnuts.

The time had come for some liquid to bind it all together. Enter the newly acquired agave syrup, leavened with oat milk and a dash of cider vinegar. I lightly combined it all into a dough, taking care that I didn't overwork it.

Nearly done! All that was needed was to roll the dough to the right thickness. About 3-4cm high would surely do it. Any thinner and the scones would become cookies. I cut them out in the requisite scone shape, and baked for a little less than 20 minutes.

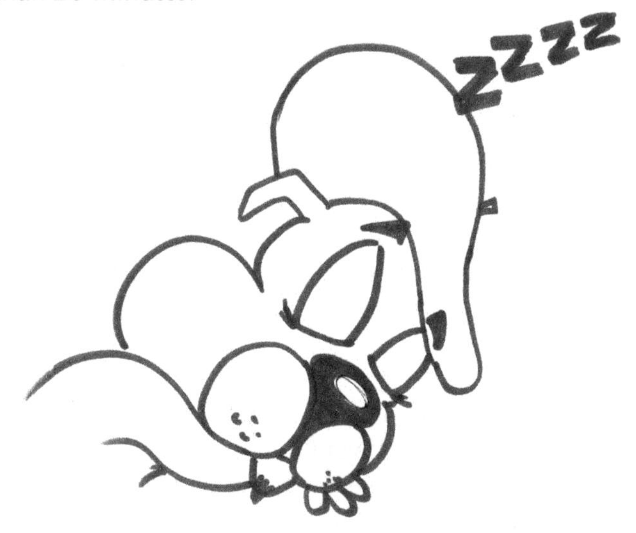

The Artist sat back, clearly feeling pleasantly sated

The Artist would surely be beside himself with glee, I thought to myself. But just to be sure, I resolved to cook an extra batch of his most favoured food. With vegan mayonnaise, we would enjoy a truly seasonal English feast: potato salad with the main course and scones with all the trimmings for pudding.

It was not certain that The Artist would even be making an

appearance that day, as we had not yet spoken. But, with his impressive intuitive senses, he arrived the very instant the scones had emerged from the oven. I should not have had any doubt!

Only a few moments later The Artist appeared in my living room and settled himself, having first attended to his dog's every need. I thought it odd that he had not remarked on the fragrant smell that clearly announced the presence of Baked Goods. But decided to say nothing at this point: the treat would be even better as a surprise.

We ate the main course. The potato salad was greeted with copious amounts of appreciative grunts, as The Artist was far too busy savouring the taste to be able to speak coherently.

The bowl was soon emptied, as he snuck an extra spoonful on his plate when he thought I was not looking. Another helping, officially his second but in all truth the third or fourth, soon followed.

The Artist sat back, clearly feeling pleasantly sated. I left him to his reverie whilst I went to the kitchen to prepare the scones. The strawberries were already sliced, just needing to be arranged artistically on each scone, with a touch of oat cream spooned over the top.

I didn't get that far, though. As a treat for the dog, I bent to add some little somethings in her bowl. I was shocked to discover a dismembered scone already there.

This act must have been perpetrated within moments of The Artist's arrival. And he had clearly deliberately resisted comment on the aroma filling my house in order to not draw attention to his crime.

29 Holiday...

The Artist had gone on holiday....

.. armed with just the essentials. Sunhat, sunglasses, oils and paintbrush.

Plus his much loved dog, of course.

He was bound to be back the following week, causing just as much chaos as always. Or so I thought...

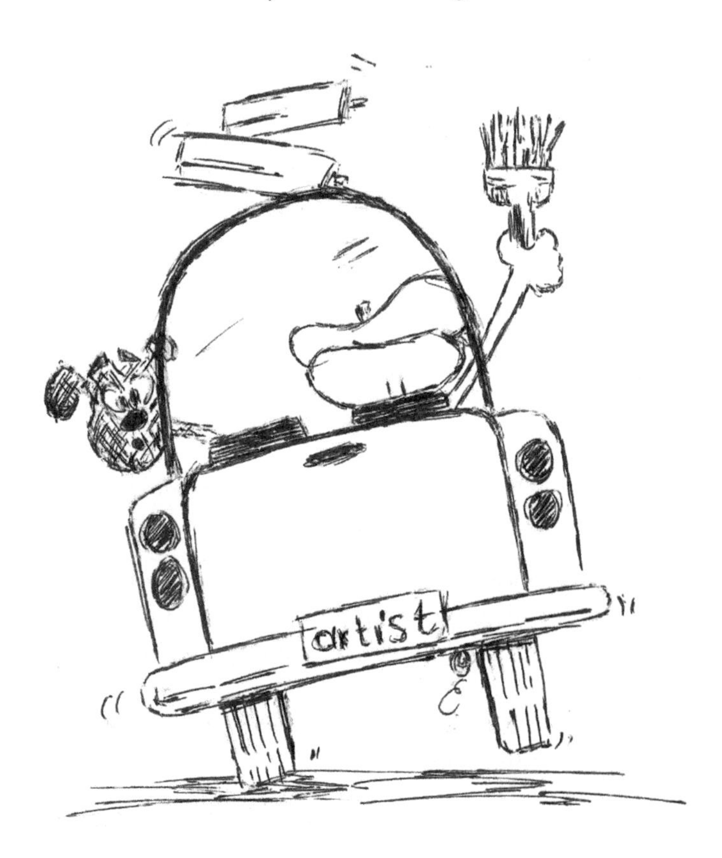

30 The Artist Refuses to Come Home...

The Artist had gone on holiday.

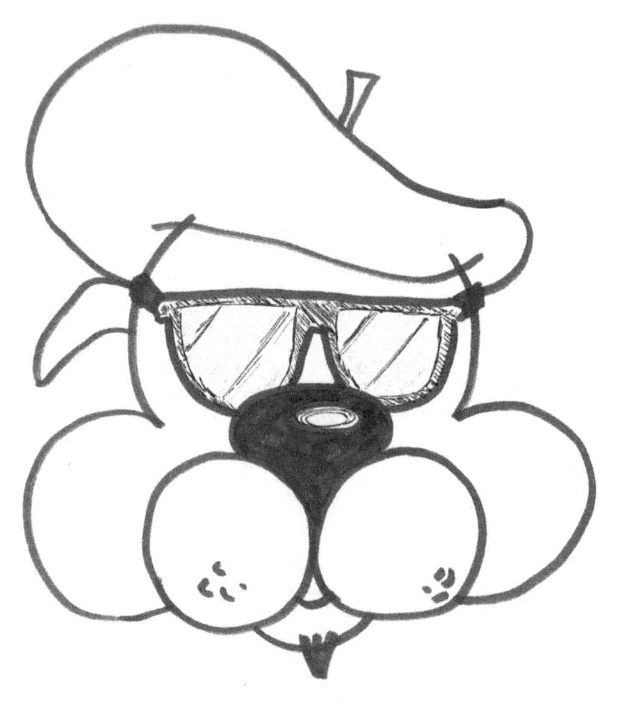

He had decided to refuse to return any time soon from his recuperation

I had received reports that he had been overheard muttering under his breath that the demands of the 'management', although effective, were quite exhausting.

Consequently he had decided to refuse to return any time soon from his recuperation.

And could not be tempted, not even for a series of little snacks.

Clearly this was serious! Not that it would ever encourage me, as the management, to rethink his gruelling schedule, of course.

But in the meantime, I allowed that he needed time in the sun (or rain, currently passing for summer here) and could be indulged a little more, so that he could wander in his own creative realms, inspired by sea, sand and nature.

At least it meant I was able to enjoy my own respite from entertaining An Artist. But he would be back, of that I was sure.

Perhaps next week? You can never tell, with An Artist...

Jacky Francis Walker

Jacky Francis Walker is a writer, editor and therapist with articles and reviews published nationally in magazines, journals and online. One of her abiding delights has been creating (and eating!) inspiring vegetarian, and now vegan, food, especially when shared with appreciative others.

She was born in London in 1956. After a first career in the computer industry in London, Jacky moved to Norfolk to become a psychotherapist, mindfulness consultant and executive coach. She currently has practices in Harley Street, the City of London and Hoxton / Shoreditch. Jacky has a particular interest in working with high achievers and people in creative fields.

In 2005 her love of arts and culture led her to set up and run a popular social group with a particular emphasis on the arts. This led to her meeting The Artist who is the inspiration for this book, and subsequently, to her ultimate dismay, becoming his manager.

Jacky shares her time between an overflowing cache of paintings, prints, photos and sculptures in Norfolk (for which she is happy to receive enquiries from art enthusiasts and collectors), her client practice in London and her husband, Geoff Francis, in Dorset.

www.theharleyconsultancy.co.uk

www.artistgeofffrancis.com

Lightning Source UK Ltd.
Milton Keynes UK
UKHW02f0939250718
326213UK00005B/70/P

9 781907 729263